MW00453476

The 5Ls
The Gift of a Balanced Life

Sal LaGreca & Mike Mannix

The 5Ls
The Gift of a Balanced Life

Sal LaGreca & Mike Mannix

ISBN - Paperback 978-1-956353-28-0
ISBN Hardback 978-1-956353-29-7
ISBN Ebook - 978-1-956353-30-3
(Motivation Champs)

The book was printed in the United States of America.

Special discount may apply on bulk quantities.
Please contact Unparalleled Performance at
info@unparalleledperformance.com to order.

Alone they have Purpose
Together they have Power

CONTENTS

The 5Ls

DEDICATIONS

To my parents, Johanna Frances and Salvatore Santo LaGreca, who not only gave me life, they saved my life; and to my son, Matthew.

—Sal LaGreca

To my children, Michael and Sarah, the center of my universe, I am so blessed to be your father and share your journey.

—Mike Mannix

"Knowing yourself is the beginning of all wisdom."
—Aristotle

INTRODUCTIONS

Sal LaGreca

Many years ago, I was asked a very simple question: How would I define success? Having just been admitted to the partnership at KPMG, I thought I was the definition of success. I had reached my goal of becoming a partner in the global firm of my choice and was on my way to personal financial freedom. My definition of success: the title and the money. You can imagine how surprised I felt when I came to the realization that there is more to life and success than just a title and money. I was both disappointed and, at the same time, eager to know how I could get these other "success" qualities in my life; what do I have to do or learn to get them? When the title and the money are gone, you better have other things in your life to help you get by and deal with all the many ups and downs of life. Having experienced decades of my own many ups and downs, I have found that having these five very simple yet essential things in my life, in a balanced fashion, has guided me through some of life's most difficult, trying, and painful times. I call them my **5Ls**.

LOVE – LAUGHTER – LABOR – LEISURE – LEAVE

Alone each has purpose; together they have power — the power to give you the needed strength to navigate through unknown and troubled waters.

This book is not a how-to book or a step-by-step self-help book. It's not a follow these five steps and you will feel like a new person book. It's a guide to a balanced life. It will show you the pathway to success in your personal and your professional life. After all these years of my own ups and downs, it is my gift to you.

Mike Mannix

I'm not going to bore you with my professional background, as I don't want this to sound like a Mike Mannix commercial. You can see that in the Bio section of the book. And if you are having a hard time sleeping one night, you can give it a read; I promise it will put you right out. But if it is okay, I would like to start by sharing a personal story that is very close to my heart and the reason why I am so passionate about the 5Ls, teaching, and helping to change people's lives for the better.

I did not grow up with money by any stretch of the imagination. I have worked my tail off for everything I have today. My goal was to be able to give my children all the things I didn't have growing up. I also wanted all the things that most people consider the standard of "success." You know what I mean, the "C-title," the nice house, the nice car, etc., etc. I worked myself almost literally to death most of my life, flying around the country and the world. I was going to be successful if it killed me, and it almost did.

My father saw how hard I was working to achieve this success and how it was driving me into the ground. He would pull me aside on a regular basis and say, "Mike, you need to stop; you are missing the real point. The true measure of success is gauged on the amount of lives you touch and leave for the better." I would always respond like a true son who was on a mission, "I hear you, Dad," and then go on my merry way. But if I'm being honest, it only halfway sunk in, if that.

My dad was a full-time pharmacist by trade, Captain of the volunteer ambulance crew (hence some of the lack of money), and a part-time Adjunct Professor teaching paramedics. It doesn't get cooler than that. He taught people how to save others' lives and all the skills needed to become an EMT or AEMT. Even though my father tried hard to have his advice sink into my thick skull, I stayed focused on what I thought was the real definition of success and finally attained everything I thought I wanted. However, I felt hollow, was miserable, and I was never around for the people that needed me most, my children. The pressure was unbelievable.

Then about fourteen years ago my world was turned upside down. I was sitting in a doctor's exam room with my father. We were there because he just didn't feel right and had this constant low-grade nausea for almost two months. It probably was longer, as my dad would never complain when he felt sick. They had put him through a battery of tests for weeks to try to get to the bottom of the issue. The doctor, whom we had known for a long time, came into the room. The look on his face said it all and made my stomach sink. He didn't beat around the bush and reviewed the results with us immediately. It was the worst diagnosis I could imagine. With a shake in his voice, the doctor looked my father in the eyes and put his hand on my father's knee and said, "Mike, you have stage four cancer. You have about two, maybe three months left to live." I thought I was going to lose it right there. I felt my eyes welling up, but I was trying to be strong for Dad. And of course, my dad being my dad, responded back with total belief, commitment, and a strength I had never heard before, "Well, that's not going to happen."

Just as a point of note, the cancer he was diagnosed with is such a rare form that only a handful of people in the last sixty-five years have contracted it. Of course, that was my dad, go big or go home. Because he is one of the very few people to have this type of cancer, he is now in a medical journal somewhere—not the kind of book you want to be in. My father, my hero, fought for his life every day for a little over two years. I watched him be taken piece by piece by this evil disease and the experimental chemotherapy they were using to hold back the cancer's progression throughout his entire body. During this time, he never complained once and tried to make an impact on the world every day. However, there quickly came a time when he could physically no longer ride the ambulance or practice pharmacy. This was so devastating for him. However, right up to the end my father taught at the college. Even if it was from a chair, he never faltered, right till his last day. This was his calling, and he was going to make a difference till the end.

When my father finally lost his courageous battle, we held a wake for three days at a very large funeral home. At every session, hundreds of people showed up. It was standing-room only, with lines out the door and around the block. It was a turnout I had never seen in my life. Beyond friends and family, people that had not seen my father going as far back as forty years came to say goodbye. Most of them were his students. Each one of them came up to me one by one with tears in their eyes, shook my hand or hugged me with true compassion. They would look almost right into my soul, and with the truest gratitude, exclaim, "Your father changed my life."

I stood there in my horrific grief in staggering awe of all the lives my father changed. That is when it hit me like a ten-ton truck. I finally had my epiphany and my biggest aha moment of my life. I knew right then and there: My father would be the most successful man I would ever meet.

Sal, Mike, The 5Ls and You

I guess you can say this book has been over thirty years in the making. Reading that, you are probably thinking, "Seriously, Sal, what took you so long?" While the 5Ls has been in my head all these years, it wasn't until a few years ago that I realized the impact it could have on people's lives on such a grand scale. I always thought it was something that I tried to have in my own life, something to help me get by when things were tough. It was just something I did for me—and I must tell you, not very well at times, as we will discuss later in this book.

So, here's how it all began. It was a beautiful summer Saturday night in Port Washington, New York, overlooking a stunning shimmering Manhasset Bay while I was entertaining a few folks at my house that the power of the 5Ls was truly exposed. That's when I met Mike Mannix. It was while I was enjoying a few beverages and admiring the sunset on the bay when my phone rang. Typically, I won't take a call when I have guests over; however, this was a call from Max, one of the top producers in my company. Now, Max would not usually be calling me on a Saturday evening, so I excused myself and took the call. He was calling to let me know he was considering resigning from the company to explore a new job opportunity. Of course, I was blown away, as it was totally unexpected. When I returned from the call, my partner, Debbie, seeing the look on my face, asked me what was wrong. I told her about Max and his decision to leave. She looked at me and said, "Well, you know that's your fifth "**L**." At that moment, Mike looked at me and said, "What is this fifth 'L' Debbie is talking about?"

I then proceeded to tell Mike the story of the **5Ls** and how I created it. I explained that when I was admitted to the partnership at KPMG over thirty years ago, at the request of the firm I attended an executive leadership conference with some top global business leaders. In one of the leadership sessions, we were all asked a very simple question: "How would you define success?" As you can imagine, the answers were all over the place. It ranged anywhere from having financial freedom to getting that coveted high level title or a position that screamed power. I have to say, there were a few answers to the success question that, at the time, I personally did not consider or that I thought weren't important enough to be part of the definition, such as being a good person or parent or a better partner or spouse. This sort of threw me off. Remember, I thought I was the definition of success. I had been admitted to the partnership of a global accounting and consulting firm—the firm that I truly wanted to be at. I was making more money than I ever had in my life. I then realized, after hearing these other things, that I began to reexamine my own definition of success. Perhaps there is more to my personal definition—more than just financial freedom and a title—to being truly successful and having balance in your life.

A few days after asking us how we all would define success, we got our feedback. It appeared that based on our collective answers there were several elements needed in life to define success. In fact, based on our group's answers, there were initially ten elements needed. Ten? I cannot tell you how surprised I was to hear this. I felt that was clearly way too many things to define a successful person. Imagine telling someone after attending a leadership development conference that one of the takeaways was that you need ten things in your life to be successful. Also, there was no way I could go back to my firm and tell them I learned (at the firm's expense) that there were ten things you need in life to be successful! Not going to happen.

I was determined to get that down to a more manageable number, a number that would be easy to keep in my brain. After pondering these ten things, I realized that several were somewhat interchangeable and clearly could be combined under a single word. So I kept working on combining the ten until I was able to narrow the list to a more manageable and personally meaningful-to-me list as well as easy to remember. I thought five accomplished both. After all, you can count them on your fingers, or toes, for that matter. Simple, right? A few of the five elements were beginning with the letter "L." I thought how cool it would be if I could get all the elements to begin with the letter "L," as this is also the first letter in my last name.

I then told Mike about my **5Ls** in life to be successful. I remember telling him, "If you have these, Mike, you've made it." His eyes lit up. What I didn't know at the time was, beyond Mike being an Executive Board Member of a global BPO, his true passion is teaching and leadership development. What I also did not know was that Mike is a well-known Adjunct Professor of leadership at New York University (NYU). He became extremely excited. While practically jumping up and down, he looked at me and stated very passionately, "Sal! That is by far the best and most impactful and true life-changing tool I have ever heard!

It is so simple and real; it's brilliant! I am a total leadership geek, have studied tools, read hundreds of books for years to help motivate and change people's lives for the better. You need to get this out there, man! You need to write a book. This could totally change people's lives for the better. People really need to hear this!" My reaction—and remember, I had just met Mike—was "Dude, you got to relax." I remember saying to Mike, "I'm not writing any books. I love to read books, but I'm not going to write a book." I think I told Mike to take it down a tad and have another beverage, as I took in his thoughts and excitement.

Mike, being a lifelong student of leadership, was the catalyst to helping me understand the true power the 5Ls could have to give people guidance and change lives for the better. I thought Mike might have had a little too many adult beverages that Saturday night, but when he showed up on my doorstep the following Monday with a whiteboard under his arm to start working on the book, I knew how much it spoke to him. And that is where it all began.

So here's a high level overview of the 5Ls.

LOVE

Without it all else fails. Without it we have nothing. Importance of *self-love*, "Oxygen Mask Theory," and the love and positive support of others.

LAUGHTER

Don't take yourself too seriously. "Stress Management" and the incredible health benefits of laughter.

LABOR

We are built and wired to work. "Passion and Purpose," the benefits of doing what you love, and self-development.

LEISURE

We need to find time to disconnect and recharge ourselves. Find your "Me Time." Clearer Minds = Better Decisions.

LEAVE

Knowing when to pivot. Adjust your sails, conquering the fear of failure, letting go of "Familiar Misery," and embracing change.

So that's the **5Ls**. Alone they have purpose; together they have power. To sum it up, the **5Ls** is a science-supported program that gives individuals the tools to navigate through difficult or challenging times in their life in order to achieve true work-life balance. It's about finding a proper balance of these **5Ls** in your life, as none of them can stand alone. It's when you are only focused on a few that life begins to unravel. We will dive deeper into each of the **5Ls** in every chapter.

Shortly after this, I asked Mike to coauthor the book with me. We also realized that we needed to get this out on a national and global basis. That is when we founded our personal, professional, and leadership development practice, Unparalleled Performance. We have been blessed to be able to get the company off the ground in a very short period of time and help thousands of people globally find true work-life balance through our trainings, seminars, and keynote speeches—The **5Ls**–The Gift of a Balanced Life.

We had nearly completed the book when the COVID-19 global pandemic crisis rocked the world and brought every one of us to our knees. The basic rule of a crisis is that you don't come out of it the same. If you get through it, you come out better or worse, but never the same. Anxiety, fear, depression, addiction, substance abuse, and divorce were at an all-time high. This contributed to a heightened focus and awareness on well-being, mental fitness, and finding true work-life balance. What we realized quickly was that the **5Ls** applies to everyone at every stage in their life and would help anyone navigate through these uncharted waters.

It is our belief that this book helps you understand that there is a need to find the correct balance of the **5Ls** in your life. You will find yourself reflecting on your own balance and the need to keep each of the 5Ls at a level that works for you.

Each one of the 5Ls is a chapter in the book. The book encompasses interviews with successful individuals who have shared their experience in one or more of the 5Ls and how it has impacted their lives. These interviews were held with corporate executives, professional athletes, high-ranking military leaders, and other high-profile personalities who have made a positive impact on people's lives. Utilizing our own combined seventy-plus years of work and life experience, along with the wisdom shared by the interviewees, we lay out real life-learning lessons and tools supported by scientific statistics.

The right balance of the 5Ls has helped individuals from all walks and in all stages of life. From students to successful leaders, the 5Ls has given them the pathway to a better, happier, and more successful life. Just some of the feedback that we have received and humbles us tremendously:

- This was fantastic! I am leaving a changed person. I cannot thank you enough.

- The 5Ls is life changing; you don't know how much I needed this!

- This was amazing! Much needed! This needs to be reinforced on a regular basis.

- I almost cried four times, as this was so helpful. I am going through so much in both my personal and professional life, and this is exactly what I needed.

- I believe the 5Ls carries a message that people need to hear. It's reassuring to know that people like Sal and Mike are out there as beacons, pointing the way forward to those wandering about in today's gloom.

- I am getting married next weekend, and I am going to change my vows to add the **5Ls**.

- Your **5Ls** is fantastic! This gave us what we desperately needed.

- Your **5Ls** is the answer to my prayers.

- The **5Ls** has made a huge impact on our organization and our initiatives to support true work-life balance and total well-being. The **5Ls**–The Gift of a Balanced Life program has received rave reviews and is being rolled out to our entire workforce.

The **5Ls** has been recognized on a global basis as an effective tool to help individuals find true work-life balance, mental fitness, as well as addressing issues with burnout. This impact has recently been highlighted in *CEOWORLD* magazine.

To help you stay focused on your own balance, at the end of each chapter, you will find ten simple questions that require a yes or no response. We call it the **5Ls** Self-Assessment Tool. As we can all agree, we need daily reminders in our life to keep us on track. If you are answering the questions honestly, and you have less than seven "Yes" answers, then you will need to work on that particular "**L**" to achieve your proper **5Ls** balance.

Our hope is that you will embrace the **5Ls**. We see the **5Ls** as our gift to you for finding true balance in work and in your life. Live the **5Ls**. Practice your balance of the **5Ls**: LOVE-LAUGHTER-LABOR-LEISURE-LEAVE. It is your pathway to personal and professional success.

In every one of our trainings, seminars, and keynote speeches we ask the participants the following:

**WHAT IF SOMEONE COULD GIVE YOU
THE GIFT OF A BALANCED LIFE?**

WHAT WOULD THAT BE WORTH TO YOU?

The answer we always receive is priceless.

This is where The **5Ls**–The Gift of a Balanced Life comes in. So let's get you started down the pathway to personal and professional success.

CHAPTER ONE

LOVE

"Love is the only force capable of transforming an enemy into a friend."
—Martin Luther King Jr.

LOVE. What a big little word. It is a key fixture in our culture, and it's the beginning of the **5Ls**. It goes back in time as far as we can remember. Love is patient. Love is kind. Without it nothing else matters. *Without love all else fails.* It makes us do crazy things, and we will sacrifice almost anything for it. Countless numbers of songs, poems, and books have been written about it. Wars have been started and ended over it. But love is much more powerful than that feeling you have for another person. It is actually one of the most powerful tools you can use in helping you achieve happiness and success.

It is true that love in our lives exists in many forms. There is love between family members, romantic love, and our love for things and objects. Love, one can argue, can make or break us as humans. In fact, it's a proven medical fact that being in love has a tendency to decrease our blood pressure and stress. Studies show that strong love relationships improve blood pressure, while being isolated from people and surrounded by strangers increases it. A recent seventy-five-year Harvard University study concluded that the quality of your close relationships directly impacts your health and quality of life. The volunteers in this study proved that from a health perspective their memory was sharper, and they far outlived their fellow volunteer subjects that had a poor support system.

The need for love is at the very core of our existence. Whatever your religious beliefs are, there is undoubtedly a reference to love in it. No matter how successful or talented one might be, if he or she is left alone and without love, they will not survive. It doesn't matter how young or old a person is, there is a fundamental need for support. There exists a need not only to love but also to be loved.

Usually when people think of the word *love*, they think of a relationship, family, or support of another. But that is where we go wrong. We should look at love in the following order:

Self-love

- Oxygen Mask Theory: You can't help others until you help yourself.
- What do you do for you?

Relationship love

- Healthy relationships bring balance.
- Surround yourself with people that support you (positive energy and people).
- No "Energy Vampires."

Love of what you do

- Your life's passion.
- Love for your team.

Love must begin with love thyself, or self-love. This must exist before you can love anyone else. Let's start with you, yes *you*. Do you truly love yourself? Do you put yourself first? Do you take care of yourself? Do you invest in yourself? Self-love is critical to everything we are going to talk about in this book. If you don't have self-love, you will never be able to have balance in your life or in the 5Ls.

~

You need to shift your thought process and put self-love in the forefront of your mind and commit to it. As Candice Corby, CEO of Cobra Legal Solutions, told us during our interview, "You have to choose self-love. Loving yourself is a choice. You must choose happiness. It doesn't come to you, and someone doesn't give it to you. Someone doesn't give you a balanced life; it's work. You get up every day and you choose a balanced life. You choose to be happy. If you don't love yourself, all else falls apart."

~

One of the most powerful lessons that anyone can learn in life is the "Oxygen Mask Theory." We know what you are thinking: "What the heck is that, and how can it change my life?" Follow us for a second. Have you ever been on a commercial airplane? Well, if you have (or haven't), before the plane is able to take off, the flight attendants go through the critical safety protocols. One of the main protocols is "In the unlikely event of a crisis and cabin depressurization, an oxygen mask will drop from the ceiling." The flight attendants will instruct you to "put the mask on yourself first, then help the person seated next to you." Stop right here. Take that in. You must help yourself first. It is not being selfish. *You cannot help anyone until you help yourself first.*

You are no good to anyone unless you take care of yourself and love yourself first. Most of us are so busy putting others and other things in front of our own needs that we get lost in the shuffle. The Oxygen Mask Theory is the visual you must embrace to drive you to take care of yourself.

Here is a story from Sal that directly speaks to this critical self-love lesson and the Oxygen Mask Theory. "In the midpart of 2018, I did not think I was unhealthy in any way, shape, or form. It was a gorgeous Sunday afternoon, and Debbie and I were having lunch with friends when I got up from my chair and quickly collapsed. I dropped like a lead balloon. Passed out. People around me actually thought I had died. I was told later that Debbie, whose mother had passed away only a week prior, was hysterically screaming, 'Sal! Oh my God! Please let him live!'

"After a series of tests, Dr. Ronnie Hirshman, a widely respected cardiologist at NYU Langone and dear friend, looked me in the eye and said, 'Unless you seriously change your diet and lifestyle, you will be having major heart surgery in the not-so-distant future.' I will never forget the look in Ronnie's or Debbie's eyes when he said that. We had discussed heart surgery before but always attempted to control my heart disease with diet, exercise, and meds. The meds I took religiously, the diet and exercise not so much.

He then strongly suggested—no, urged me—to change my lifestyle and go on a whole food, plant-based diet. Which I did. Really not a diet but a change in how I live. A true lifestyle change. For me, really something that never entered my mind and was very hard to do.

"You see, I grew up in a household eating meats of all kinds every day. My father owned a butcher shop, so we ate all kinds of beef, chicken, pork, whatever and whenever we wanted. I thought long and hard about this major change in my life. But more importantly, I thought about my wonderful son, Matthew, and my daughter-in-law, ToniAnn; my four beautiful grandchildren, Giuliana, Charlie, Tommy, and Ellie; and about Debbie and her children, Brett and Grace. How can I do this to my family, the people I love? I thought, *No matter what it takes I will change.* This is where self-love comes smashing through and slaps you upside the head. *Wake up, Sal! Love thyself and do what needs to be done to be available to love others and have them love you back.*"

Let's now have a quick discussion about *self-love* and *self-sacrifice.*

When someone goes through life with a self-sacrificing approach, they miss out on the things they personally want to do for themselves and perhaps the things that are more important to them. In other words, they sacrifice, or give up, on their own self-love. In many cases, this might include a parent/child relationship where the child or the parent will sacrifice something he or she wants so as not to disappoint the other person. This is because they fear the rejection or disappointment, and self-love takes a back seat.

One example that hits home for Sal had to do with the relationship with his beautiful and loving mother, Johanna

Frances LaGreca. As Sal tells the story, "When I was born, it was a life and death situation because of a medical emergency called blue baby syndrome. It involves an Rh-negative blood factor in the mother that causes cyanosis in the infant, usually from a congenital heart defect in which venous and arterial blood are comingled. The Rh disease occurs during pregnancy. It happens when the Rh factors in the mom's and baby's blood don't match. If the Rh-negative mother has been sensitized to Rh-positive blood, her immune system will make antibodies to attack her baby. A high percentage of methemoglobin in the blood can lead to death.

"From what my parents told me, as a Catholic, this apparent death situation required an emergency baptism and administration of the Catholic last rites. This is the reason my name is the same as my dad's, Salvatore. Apparently, without my parents in the room during the emergency baptism and not knowing what name my parents chose for me, the standard procedure was to use the father's name if it is a boy and the mother's if it's a girl. As a result of my condition, my mother made a promise to God that if I were to live, she would offer my life up to God and the Catholic church. Growing up, I was constantly reminded that my life belonged to the Catholic church.

"When it was time for my graduation from St. Kevin's, my Catholic elementary school in Flushing, New York, at the ripe young age of fourteen I was faced with the decision as to what high school I would choose to attend. Of course, it would have to be a Catholic high school. Remember, I was destined to become a priest. Not really destined, but rather my mother's pledge to God for saving my life. At that time, there were several good Catholic school choices, such as Bishop Riley, Holy Cross, Archbishop Molly, Monsignor McClancy, just to name a few. My graduating class was quite split as to what school they would attend.

"Here's where the fun begins. Of course, my mother had another idea regarding high school for Sal. How about the Catholic high school called Cathedral Preparatory Seminary? Cathedral Prep is a Catholic high school you would attend because you have a desire or a calling to the Catholic priesthood. Or in my case, it was because my mother dedicated my life to God and the Catholic church and wanted me to be a priest. And of course, so as not to disappoint my mother, I attended Cathedral Prep in Elmhurst, New York—for me at the time, two buses and two trains from our house. Needless to say, my mother was quite pleased and extremely happy. I got news for you: I wasn't. Sorry, Father Troike; I was miserable.

"My stay at Cathedral Prep didn't last. I left after one year and enrolled in my original school of choice, Bishop Riley High School, where half my grammar school classmates and friends were. Mom was not happy; I was, though. But I must tell you, I felt like my world was caving in, as I disappointed my mother. While I was happy and felt a sense of freedom, the guilt was such a burden. So what I did by leaving Cathedral Prep was to essentially replace self-sacrifice with self-love. It was not easy. The burden of guilt is powerful. Such a weight. But I was finally taking care of my own needs, the classic Oxygen Mask approach to self-love and to life that we talked about earlier in this chapter. Help yourself first so you can then help others.

"It was surely the beginning of the end of my self-sacrificing days. Believe me, it was not easy. Goodbye to self-sacrifice and hello to self-love. That's real love. And that's where it should start, with you."

A critical mistake that people make when it comes to self-love is putting everything and everyone ahead of themselves. This can have a devastating impact on one's health and well-being. We certainly have seen that in the healthcare industry and frontline workers.

A critical component to self-love is finding time for yourself that gives you joy and fuel for your soul. You need to be asking yourself every day, "What am I doing for me today?" Not once or twice a week, every single day. We don't care where you put it, but write that question down and put it somewhere you will see it throughout the day so it reminds you. We know this might sound crazy, but you are worth it!

You will note throughout the book that the 5Ls overlap, intertwine, and *always work together* in a balanced fashion to guide you through whatever you are dealing with. They are not a list, but rather a circle with no end and no beginning. Remember, alone they have purpose; together they have power.

As parents, partners, employees, leaders, and as individuals, not taking care of ourselves or loving oneself first is detrimental to your mental and physical well-being. It is also the key reason why people don't succeed in life at their jobs, in relationships, or in finding true happiness. It cannot be repeated enough: You need to do something for *you* every single day.

After self-love, next you need the proper love relationships in your life. You need to surround yourself with people that will give you true emotional sustenance. If you don't have them, *you need to find them.* You need to be around people that lift you up and have your best interests at heart.

You also need to remove or lessen the time with the ones that bring you down, the ones that take and don't really give back. This can be very difficult, as these negative influences could be your family, your partner, or could be friends that you have known most of your life. You must identify what we refer to as "Energy Vampires," and lessen their impact on your life quickly. Energy Vampires are just that; they suck the life out of you, only thinking of themselves, putting you down, or making the relationship a one-way street. The ones that are hardest to spot are the part-time Energy Vampires. They are not as consistent in this practice. However, they can be even more dangerous, as you will ride the wave with them longer because it's harder to see. Make no mistake; you cannot have this in your life and be successful. Get rid of the straws in your life, the people that take out of you. You need people that are like pitchers, ones that pour in.

We know some very successful people that have made a lot of money and are in high-level positions but are missing the proper personal support. If you ask them if they are truly happy and feel successful, even though they have accomplished so much, they will say without blinking an eye, "No!" They are missing important personal support relationships, people that they trust, support them, and love them unconditionally without an agenda. Having these critical relationships as part of your life impacts every—and we mean *every*—part of your ability to be happy, effective, and successful.

Another essential part of love is loving what you do and who you do it with. Think about it: You spend most of your waking hours some days with the people you work with. If you do not like them or what you do, you are destined to be miserable. Believe us: People can tell when you are faking it. They will only follow someone that they know has their best interest at heart.

Let's also talk about how love can influence and have a very positive impact on a team's performance and their ability to successfully get things done. Being a truly effective leader is also about having a servant's mentality: giving of oneself and the belief they are there to serve their team, not the other way around. This is called "Servant Leadership." However, it is important to note that *you do not need to be in charge of a team or company to be a leader.* A leader is anyone who sets a good example and impacts people's lives for the better. You need to be a leader in both your home and in your work life. Great and successful leaders aren't driven to lead but to serve—which is a true expression of love. It's never about the role; it's about the goal.

~

This was reinforced by Candice Corby during our recent interview. She is a passionate Servant Leader that told us, "Success for me is leaving a person, place, industry, or a heart better than you found it. You want to touch a person and plant a seed. You want to plant a thought in somebody's mind to help them grow and do something better."

~

Another perfect example of this came out of our interview with Randell (Rande) Bynum, CEO Girl Scouts of Nassau County, New York, and could not have been said any more clearly: "I really enjoy leadership and try to get better at it every day. I believe in being a compassionate leader. To do this you need to truly care about people. A leader is not always in the front. A leader needs to be aligned with the group and jump in when needed. I am a team player that can be in the mix but can switch to make the high-level decisions for the good of the whole. A leader is not being a boss. A blazer does not make you a boss. Listening to your staff, engaging with your team, showing that you care, being compassionate with your staff, and focusing on their best interests makes you a leader."

~

Following up on Rande Bynum's comment that true leaders must be authentic and serve their team is the definition of true servant leadership. Getting to your team's heart is the key to authentic and successful leadership. This applies to both your personal and professional life.

Here is a quick story where Mike learned the hard way the critical need for a leader to get to the team's heart. "Early on in my career, I made the catastrophic mistake of thinking that I knew how to motivate a team by being a nice guy, understanding basic blocking and tackling, and from my past track record with my prior team. This story all started when a good friend of mine had begun working for this fast-growing company and reached out to me one day. She called me up and said, 'Hey Mike. I found this tremendous opportunity for you. There is an opening at my company, and you would be perfect for the role.' This, of course, immediately intrigued me. I responded with, 'I would love to interview for the position, but I don't have any experience in the industry.' She said, 'Not a problem at all. You are a total cultural fit, and I already told them all about you. Can you take a call with the President next week?' So, of course, I made myself available.

"The call went better than I could have imagined, and I was immediately blown away by this incredibly dynamic executive. She was everything that I aspired to be in a leader, and I desperately wanted to learn from her. Over the next few weeks, I went through a gauntlet of interviews with her management team. This was no easy feat and nerve racking to say the least.

"A few days after the last interview my phone rang. I recognized the number immediately. It was the President of the company! I was so excited but let it ring two or three times (so as not to look too eager) and tried to answer as calmly as possible: 'This is Mike.' Lame, I know, but this is what came out of my mouth. She didn't waste any time and said, 'Hi Mike. I have to tell you, you really impressed my team. We would love to have you join the company. When can you start? I am really looking forward to working with you.' I was on cloud nine but had a lot to consider. This was a very scary jump for me, as my first child, Michael, was just born; my wife at the time was a stay-at-home mom, and this job was in a totally different industry. I thought long and hard, but I bit the bullet. I left my job of eight years and took that leap as the new leader of a critical division. What I wasn't told was, the person I was replacing was loved—and when I say loved, I mean capital L-O-V-E-D by his team— but had recently been promoted to a new role. However, at the ripe old age of twenty-nine, I came in thinking I knew it all on how to manage and inspire teams, as I had been so successful in my prior job. As you can tell, I was very impressed with myself then. I was totally clueless.

"About thirty days after starting, the President called me into her office. She looked at me and said, 'So how is it going?' Being the positive person I am, I responded with, 'It's going great!' I then proceeded to tell her with pride about all the new process improvements I was making and how I increased profits in the short time I was there. She then asked me a question I will never forget. She said, 'Do you think that is your team out there?' I responded with a big fat 'Yes! They love me!' and then talked about all the things I was doing with them to make them more efficient.

"What I did not know at that time was that she had held private meetings with my entire staff, and the feedback was *not* good, to say the least.

"She immediately proceeded to roll her chair quickly up to me, got about two inches from my face, and while pointing her finger an inch from my nose, stated very loudly, 'No, they are not! You haven't gotten to their hearts; they won't stand up for you, and you are blowing it, Mannix! You need to find out what makes them tick, and fast. You need to quickly get to know them as people; then you might have a chance. You have got thirty days to fix it! Now get out of my office!'

"I could feel the blood drain out of my face, and I came close to throwing up in her garbage pail. I was sitting in a pool of sweat in front of the person I desperately wanted to learn from and impress and was being told I was blowing it. So once I could feel my legs again, I stood up with my tail tucked between my legs, and I walked out the door. I can only imagine what I looked like leaving her office; I could barely breathe.

"I thought to myself, *I got to figure this out fast or I'm done*. All that was going through my mind was that I had way too much riding on this new job. So I got busy getting to know my team as individuals. I took them out to lunch individually and took them out to dinner as a team. I also held one-on-one touchpoints and jumped into the day-to-day with them, never asking them to do something I would not do myself. Also—and a very important note—I brought LAUGHTER and LEISURE into the workplace. I made sure we did not take ourselves too seriously and introduced taking time out to have fun and bond as a team.

"So here is the point of this story: After doing a lot of research on how to get under the surface and how to get to know people at a deeper level, and then using the information I attained in the individual meetings with my team, I formed four very simple questions to really get to know someone. Have you ever heard the term 'tip of the iceberg'? Here is what it boils down to: If you are a Discovery Channel junky like me, you would have learned that 80–90 percent of an iceberg is under the surface. So in reality, you are only seeing very little of that iceberg's magnitude. It is the same with people. Let's stop here for a quick second. Most of the time when we deal with people, we only learn superficial information, just what you can see on the surface. What you might not realize is, this is true in both your personal and professional life. This is a real miss, and you will never be truly successful in any part of your life without understanding what makes someone tick.

"These four basic questions will give you an insight and a view under the surface that you would never get unless you ask. They are as follows:

- **What are you passionate about?**

- **What motivates you?**

- **How do you like to be communicated to?**

- **How do you like to be managed?**

"Fast-forward thirty days. The President called me back into her office. My heart was racing, and beads of sweat started to form on my forehead. This time she didn't waste a second, looked me in the eyes and asked again in a stern voice, 'So do you think that's your team out there, Mr. Mannix?' I mustered up everything in me, sat erect in my chair, and responded with a confident, 'Yes. I really believe they are now.' I then told her about the four questions I created to get under the surface with the team, everything I did to get to their hearts, to motivate them, and was not sure what else I could do better. Once again, she rolled her chair up to me. I could feel my lunch coming up and thought I was going to lose it right there. She got right up to my face and stated loudly, 'You're right! That is your team out there. Good job, Mannix. Nicely done. Keep up the good work!' Then she smiled and, while laughing, finished with, 'Now get out of my office.'

"This team went on to win multiple awards and quickly became the highest producers of the company, generating the best margins of any division. To this day, I have continued to use this technique on how to get to know people and consistently reap similar results in both my personal and professional life.

"These simple questions will give you an insight into what really matters to the person you are speaking with. I have now used them for my entire career to truly understand someone. I will use them during interviews or anytime new members joined my team. It is the key to finding out quickly what makes people tick. You can also use them in your personal life as well to understand someone so you can have a better relationship. And here is the bottom line on why they are applicable to both:

Passion is what drives us as people. It is what we care about deep down at our core. If you know what someone is passionate about, you can connect with them on a totally different level.

People are motivated by many different things: money, praise, recognition, growth, and so on. Knowing this is key to managing or inspiring your team and taking their performance to the next level.

Communication is key. Knowing what medium or how someone processes information best will yield unparalleled results. Some people respond better to email, some a phone call or text, some like a lot of detail, and others want just the facts. Pure example: If I call my daughter on her cell, she usually won't answer. However, if I send a text, I will get an immediate response. It is just how she communicates.

People respond to different management styles. Knowing what management style they respond to is one of the most important management tools. Some people like to be micromanaged, given lots of detail and guidance, while others like to be macromanaged and left to their own devices with little supervision to reach the goal. Others like a little of both. If you use the wrong style on someone, you will demotivate them and lose them quickly.

"Out of my initial failure, and with the tough love of my mentor, Kate, came one of the biggest learning lessons that changed the trajectory of my entire career and as well as my personal relationships. To be a truly effective and inspiring leader, you need to get to your team's hearts. Find out what they *love*, what *motivates* them, how they like to *communicate* and be *managed*; most of all, show that you care about them. It doesn't need to be a big or grandiose gesture either. It's the little things you do for someone that shows them you truly care. Like saying 'Thank you,' 'Great job,' or 'You are really making an impact.' Also, giving little things like a small gift card or even a thank you card that you handwrote will totally change someone's day.

"Here is a really easy one that most people sadly don't think about and can make a tremendous impact and takes only thirty seconds out of your day. We all have this amazing cool app on our phones called a calendar. Find out the birthdays of your team members and the important people in your life. Put them in your phone and set a reminder for it to go off every year. When it does, take a few seconds to wish that person a happy birthday. What you may not realize is that when you say 'Happy Birthday' to someone, you are recognizing the day they came into the world and made it a better place. You are acknowledging the importance of their existence. This small act touches people on a personal and psychological level more than you might understand. It truly is all about the little things in both your personal and professional life that make all the difference to show you truly care."

~

As Gloria Greco, retired Senior Risk Management Executive Bank of America and CCO Merrill Lynch, told us very clearly, "People want to feel valued. Making people feel this way is one of the keys to success."

~

Another example of love for your team and true authentic leadership is a story told to us by Jim Heekin, chairman and CEO of Grey Global Group, an advertising and marketing communications company. During Jim's interview for this book, he shared a story about when Grey was preparing for a presentation to Gillette. As they say, timing is everything. As the Grey team was getting close to the presentation date, the devastating hurricane, Superstorm Sandy, hit the East Coast in 2012, and New York City in particular, pretty hard. It inflicted nearly $70 billion in damages, one of the deadliest, destructive, and most costly storms. Most of NYC lost power and, as you can imagine, certainly not a comfy environment to be in as you are preparing for a multimillion-dollar advertising and marketing pitch. As the Grey team was huddled in a rented basement of a nearby hotel—with a working generator—Jim was right there in it with his team every step of the way. As Jim said, "The team was working hard as hell. So you can say we had LABOR, we had LAUGHTER, and we certainly had LOVE. Love what you do. And we did. Love galvanized this group of people. Love is the driver of the 5Ls; it's what facilitates all the others. It ignites all those other critical components, and if you don't love yourself, you cannot be a successful leader." As Jim so eloquently stated, "Love drives the whole bus, Sal; no bullshit. I believe that to the bottom of my soul. I love competing, building teams and competing. Love winning." Grey won the Gillette business and enjoyed their LEISURE thereafter.

~

In another interview, we had the distinct honor to speak with retired Four-Star General US Army, David Perkins. General Perkins spent most of his adult life in the service of our country and saw some really terrible things. What we didn't know at the time of the interview was that General Perkins was one of the direct contributors and publisher (as the TRADOC Commander) in the development and writing of the US Army's *Leadership Development Manual FM 6-22*. So we literally had the person that wrote the book on leadership sitting in front of us. We went over the 5Ls with him, and he loved it all. However, during the interview, the "L" that spoke to him the most was LOVE. He then proceeded to tell us a story about one of his team members that came up to him many years ago.

One day a corporal stopped him, saluted, and said, "Sir! I need to tell you something, Sir!" General Perkins responded, "Of course, Corporal, what is it?" He replied, "The team and I need to let you know that whenever we would get into horrible firefights with the bullets flying and no way out, and we thought it was the end, we would track your call sign, Spartan 6. Once we heard this on the radio and knew you were on the way to get us out, we would take a deep breath and know deep down not to be afraid and that we were going to make it. It always seemed that when things got at their worst, you would show up. We always knew you cared about us and would do anything to get us out."

General Perkins looked at us with a tear in his eye—which also made *us* well up—and said, "When your team knows you care about them, they can accomplish anything." We still get goose bumps when we think about this story. It speaks to the real core of LOVE.

~

Now, let's talks about the importance of forgiveness as it relates to love. Sal would say, "I am reminded about another thought with respect to love from my high school story, and it's the act of forgiveness. I needed to forgive my mother for dedicating my life to the church and her wish and desire for me to become a Catholic priest." *Forgiveness is one of the greatest expressions of love.* Love for yourself and the one you are forgiving—even if the one you are forgiving is yourself. No matter how hard it is, you must dig deep down and truly forgive. You must find the courage and strength to forgive someone—or even yourself, for that matter—for your self-love and well-being. Holding on to anger and regret eats at you like a cancer. You need to let it go and move forward or it will literally destroy you from the inside. Once the sincere apology has been made, you let it go, move on, and learn from it. Period.

A recent Johns Hopkins study showed that holding on to resentment, hate, anger, regret, and not releasing this to forgiveness causes heart disease, high blood pressure, depression, post-traumatic stress disorder (PTSD) as well as multiple other mental health issues.

Forgiveness, you can say, is where LOVE, LAUGHTER, LABOR, LEISURE, and LEAVE intersect. Take this to heart. You need to forgive (LOVE) to bring the joy back (LAUGHTER), work hard at it (LABOR) so you can return to your comfort zone (LEISURE) and be able to put it behind you (LEAVE).

Having *selfless love* is also another beautiful way of showing true love. Selfless love sometimes includes changing your own life plans or putting them on hold for a bit because someone needs your support. It may not be what you thought it would be, but you know your partner, family member, or friend needs you more than ever. So you change your own plans and perhaps your dreams to be there for them when they need you most. That is not self-sacrifice; that is selfless love.

~

This happened to Winston Henderson, VP and General Counsel of Scientific. In our interview, he described how the passing of his brother had him take on a new role with his brother's children. "I probably never told anybody this story. I had two brothers. Unfortunately, both have passed. My oldest brother was eleven years older than me. He, unfortunately, passed at the age of forty-one, leaving behind his wife and four kids. When this happened, I immediately went from being a thirty-year-old bachelor to taking on a much more substantial role in my nephews' lives in various ways. While I could never replace my brother, you want them to see and feel your love as much as possible.

"The oldest was sixteen at the time, and the youngest was eight. The oldest was able to comprehend the loss more and hit him harder than the others. While doing my best to guide and console him in his grief, I would explain that almost everybody has something in life that screws them up and works against them. If the thing that throws you out of balance is the absence of your father (because you loved him so much), that's actually a good thing. You were blessed to have him and be able to feel that level of love.

"I think the lesson I learned is that to go fully into love means risk, because the loss of that means you will experience deep hurt. So when you see someone who loses a loved one and it makes them upset, that is a good thing, because it was so worth it. To have it hurt deeply meant they had loved deeply. Whether you think it's spiritual, physiological, or biochemical, these things that we experience as love, who knows what it truly is. But my theory is that these things are true and make life worth living."

~

We want to share with you a true love story from our interview with former Major League Baseball player Tommy John. He spoke to us about a tragic accident involving his son Travis. "My son Travis fell out of a third-story window in 1981, and he was in the hospital for a month. He was in a coma for seventeen days. When Travis was out of the hospital and recovered, Mr. Steinbrenner asked him if he wanted to throw out the first pitch of a playoff game. I was pitching that game and knew it would be too emotional for me. So I asked Reggie Jackson if he would take my son out to the mound to throw out the pitch. After Travis threw out the first ball, and it was a strike, Reggie picked him up and held him as high as he could and turns him around Yankee stadium. There were sixty-four thousand people chanting, 'Travis, Travis, Travis.' I am crying my eyes out. So I went to the umpire and said, 'I can't see because I'm crying so hard. Can you just give me the outside corner?' He said, 'No problem, because I can't see either, as I'm crying too!' I realized all that mattered was my son was being healthy and the countless number of times I'll be able to show my love for him."

~

Candice Corby summed up the power of love perfectly. "Out of all the **Ls**, LOVE speaks to me the most. I think you need to love what you do, love your work, and love your home life. If you focus on love, all the other Ls come along with it. So if you choose love, you have chosen balance."

~

A final thought with respect to self-love and the Oxygen Mask Theory as it relates to Mike's life as a caretaker. "What I didn't mention in the introduction is, the year that I lost my father to cancer, my marriage failed, and I became a single dad all at the same time. To say this was the scariest and darkest point in my life would be an understatement. At the time, I was the ultimate self-sacrificer, or what is called a caretaker. I put everyone and their needs above myself. I took care of people, I fixed their problems or their bad situations, and made them better."

Does this sound like something you do? What I didn't realize is that this self-sacrifice and caretaker approach is the death blow to self-love.

"During this very dark time, when I felt like everything was falling apart, I was scared out of my mind. I was depressed and didn't know which way to turn. I was what you would call a 'hot mess.' There were days that I didn't want to get out of bed. I would open my eyes every morning with my stomach sick from fear and anxiety about the day ahead, but failure was not an option. I would lay there saying to myself, *Get up, Mannix. Your two beautiful and amazing children are counting on you; they didn't ask for this, and you can't let them down. Now get your ass out of bed!* I realized quickly that I couldn't do this on my own; I just didn't know how. Nor did I have the tools. I was so lost, and there were times I was just so overwhelmed I did nothing. Knowing this was not going to work, I got myself professional help.

"I had never been to a therapist for myself and didn't know what to expect. To be honest, it took a lot for me to go, as I thought I should be able to fix myself on my own. I would disapprovingly look in the mirror and say, 'You should be better and stronger than this.' Does that sound familiar? I also thought to myself, *How will people look at me if I am seeing a shrink?* I hate that term, by the way. I was an Executive Board Member of a big company at this point in my career and was scared that people would find out I was getting professional help. I would hesitate going to see someone, as thoughts would race through my mind: *What if people find out? What would they think? Would they lose confidence in me? Would it jeopardize my job?* On and on that crap would ruminate in my head. I would just relentlessly beat myself up for not being strong enough to fix myself.

"I was getting my kids ready for school one morning

when I was dressing my daughter, who was seven at the time. She looked at me, put her hand on my cheek, tilted her head, and said softly, 'Are you okay, Daddy?' I replied, 'Why, Bug?' 'Bug' is my nickname for my daughter, a term of endearment, as she is my love bug. In her sweet, innocent little voice, she said, 'Your eyes are watery. Were you crying, Daddy?' I quickly collected myself, turned my head away, wiped my eyes, and turned back to her and said, 'Daddy is okay, sweetheart. Please don't worry. Now let's braid your pretty hair.' This rocked me to my core. I needed to get over myself and that BS quickly and get support and get it now. For the record, I now know and preach that getting help should never be something to be ashamed of. It doesn't mean you are weak. It actually means you are smart and strong enough to admit you don't know it all and that you need help.

"I pulled up to the therapist's office the first night. I'm not sure how long I just sat there in my car, but I finally mustered up my strength and headed in. I was greeted by an older gentleman with a very kind demeanor. He was the picture of what you might think a therapist would look like. He had silver hair, dark-framed glasses, white shirt, vest, and slacks. He welcomed me in and sat me down in a comfortable leather chair. The room was very calming. Soft classical music was playing, and all of his credentials lined the walls in beautiful frames. I immediately felt safe. After some small talk he asked why I was there. I went into everything I just described—from losing my father to becoming a single dad, my high-stress job, and that I needed to be there to take care of others, especially my children. As I told him, the emotions overwhelmed me. My eyes watered, and I just sat there silently sobbing. He looked up from his pad and asked me a question that was so foreign to me at the time: 'What do you do for you, Mike?' I responded, 'I don't understand the question.' Patiently, he said it again: 'What do you do for you? What time do you spend on you to help you?' Of course I replied, 'Nothing. There is no time for me.'

"Now, I am not going to bore you with all the details of the rest of the session, but this is when I first learned the thought process that would save my life and my children's: the Oxygen Mask Theory.

"I had to realize I needed to find things for me, things that would give me mental and emotional fuel. The sheer pressure of what I was going through drained every part of my being. Have you ever felt like that, where you were just totally mentally and physically exhausted? I wouldn't wish this on my worst enemy. It is crippling in every sense of the word. So now for the first time in my life, I needed to take care of myself first. This was a totally foreign concept to me, as that was not the way I was wired. But this old way of thinking had to change. There was no choice in the matter; my precious children deserved more. It was time to focus on my own mental wellness and well-being in order to be the parent my children should have in their life.

"This was no small feat, but I took it one step and one day at a time. First thing to define was what would be my true Me Time. We will go deeper into what this is in the LEISURE chapter. For my spirit, I focused on my faith. I prayed harder than ever. I have always prayed, but I really kicked it up a notch. Thank God for my faith, as it gave me comfort. It also gave me the courage I needed just to get out of bed and face the day. For my body and mind, I would exercise, do something physical to release the negative energy. I also would get a babysitter from time to time just to get out with family or friends, people that would lift me up. You know what I mean, real true friends. This was critical; and I can't tell you how grateful I am for the people that were by my side. You know who you are, and I love you all and can never thank you enough.

"I worked hard every day to stay focused on my mental and physical health. Making sure to keep the Oxygen Mask Theory in the forefront of my mind at all times was the only way I was able to be a truly good parent to my children. Now I'm not saying I didn't have some bad days, but I am saying that this was what got me to where I am today. I can tell you from firsthand experience that taking care of myself first has had a profound impact on my life. I will go deeper into this time in my life in the later chapters."

If you walk away with anything from this chapter, at a minimum, take away this key point: You need LOVE in your life in all the ways and the in order we discussed: self-love, relationship love, and love of what you do. Because without LOVE, all else fails. It has been written that love is the *bond of perfection*.

As we mentioned, humans are very visual creatures. Subconsciously, we will not only relate an emotion to a word we hear but a color as well. We will ask this question for each "L" at the end of every chapter. What color comes to mind when you hear the word *Love*? Now hold on to that color, as it will all come together when you get to the LEAVE chapter.

∼

The following is part of our **5Ls** Self-Assessment Tool. There will be one of these self-assessments at the end of each chapter for each of the **Ls**. Find a quiet moment and answer yes or no to these ten simple questions as honestly as you can. If the question is something you are on the fence about or have just somewhat in your life, then the answer should be "No." If you have less than seven "Yes" answers, that is an indicator that you need to work on this particular "L" to find your **5Ls** balance.

LOVE

"Y"	"N"	
		Do I put my oxygen mask on every day (Self-Love)?
		Do I have an attitude of gratitude?
		Do I feel I am worth it; do I love who I am?
		Do I have the right people in my life; people who lift me up?
		Do I forgive myself for feeling down?
		Do I realize that I should never settle for less than I deserve?
		Do I forgive people that I feel have wronged me?
		Do I bet on myself to win?
		Do I reward myself?
		Do I tell the special people in my life "I love you" enough?

CHAPTER TWO

—

LAUGHTER

"If one has no sense of humor, one is in trouble."
—Betty White

LAUGHTER is a key element to a balanced and healthy life. *Not taking yourself or life too seriously* is critical to good health and achieving the success you are looking to attain. To be able to find true balance in your life, you must be able to laugh at yourself.

Well, talk about laughing at yourself and not taking yourself too seriously! This LAUGHTER approach of not taking yourself too seriously became very clear for Sal during one of his early work experiences.

"I was a first-year accountant at a firm called Peat Marwick Mitchell & Co., the predecessor firm to today's KPMG. I remember it pretty clearly. I was assigned to the team that was performing the annual audit of the Irving Trust Company down on Wall Street. I was a staff accountant reporting directly to the senior manager, who I will call Ed. Ed's next step in the firm was to become a partner, and it was very clear that he was certain to be admitted to the partnership. Ed had it all, and I wanted to be like him. My goal was to be admitted to the partnership as well. Ed wore suspenders, or braces. I wore a belt. I thought that Ed's suspenders were the coolest thing and had a very serious and professional appearance to them. So I did a little research and found the best store to go to and dress for success. I had heard of the place. I wasn't sure if I had heard my mother mention it or if it was from a Mary McCarthy short story, but it sounded serious enough: Brooks Brothers. So I purchased my first pair of suspenders, navy blue in color, and I felt serious and very professional.

"I knew that when Ed would see me, he would be impressed. So I headed into the city feeling and looking damn good. I will never forget his face when he saw me wearing my new navy blue suspenders *and* my old belt. Yes, belt and suspenders. Ed liked the suspenders and was keen to remark about the overkill here in keeping my pants from falling off. He had a good laugh. I didn't at first, but later I sure did, and laughed pretty hard. A good example of not taking myself too seriously."

~

Oliver (Ollie) J. Crom, retired Chairman of Dale Carnegie, once told us, "My father always said, 'Don't take yourself too seriously; no one gets out of this life alive.'"

~

Talking about not taking yourself too seriously, how about growing up in an Italian family with dozens of Italian male cousins. As Sal will say, "You learn at a very young age that you definitely don't take your given name seriously. How could you when everyone in your family from day one calls you by a different name. My given name is Salvatore, but my whole life I was called 'Sally' or 'Sally boy.' My brother's name is John, but he's known to this day as 'Johnny boy.' Just ask my gifted cousin and author, Paul LaGreca, or 'Paulie,' what it was like growing up in a house with five brothers who were never referred to by their given names. There was Charlie, Eddie, Johnny, Tommy, and Jaimie. Silly, but it made you feel loved, a real term of endearment. The only time you were called by your given name was when you did something wrong, your mother would call you by your full given name, like 'Salvatore LaGreca! Get over here now!' You knew you were in trouble."

~

Here is a snippet on this subject from our interview with Richard Catalano, a dear, old friend of Sal's and successful entrepreneur. He told us the following story: "I did a yoga class in NYC. You had to take this class in a martial arts uniform. They brought in a yin and yang doctor one day, and he said that the first thing you should do every day is make ten funny faces at yourself in the mirror, and I promise you will have a good day. What most people do is look in the mirror and look to improve themselves as opposed to having fun with it. So take time to laugh at yourself, and do not take yourself too seriously." So simple but worth the effort.

~

Being able to laugh at yourself is so important in life. As Mike recalls, "Sal recently reminded me of a totally true story

I experienced that still makes my sides hurt. He said, 'Mike, you *have* to put the airplane story in the book. It's too good, bro!'" So you can thank Sal for this one. Okay, Mr. LaGreca, this one's for you. Now mind you, I didn't find it so funny at the time, but I hope you enjoy it as much as my friends do.

"It was the middle of January here in New York with frigid winds, snow, and ice. I had to fly out in two days for a very important board meeting in London. I hadn't felt good for about two or three days, when my throat started to feel like it was on fire. Just swallowing felt like razorblades. Knowing I had to fly in forty-eight hours, I called my doctor and begged to get in for an appointment. He fit me in. Sitting on the exam table, the doctor looks down my throat and says the two words you never want to hear from a physician, 'Oh boy...' followed by 'not good.' I replied with, 'Doc, I have to fly in two days. I can't miss this meeting. All the global heads will be there.' He rolled his eyes at me and replied, 'You never learn, do you, Mike? Well, my friend, you have strep throat. If you take the antibiotic I'm going to give you, you won't be contagious in forty-eight hours, so I guess you can fly.'

"Fast forward two days later of taking the medication. I wake up that morning at 4:00 a.m., as a car is coming to pick me up to take me to the airport for a 7:00 a.m. flight. I feel like hell: achy, throat still hurts; but I say to myself (like the moron I am), *Well, the doc said I could fly.* Car picks me up. I get to the airport, and I get on the plane. I'm thinking, *Well, at least I can sleep on the flight.* This is about a seven-to-eight-hour trip, so I'm looking forward to closing my eyes. I put in my earplugs, grab a blanket, and snuggle in.

"About ninety minutes into the flight, I wake up with

my mouth and throat as dry as a desert. I have a taste in my mouth that can only be described as burnt chutney and hair. As I gaze up, I see the flight attendant walking up the aisle with a tray of water and juices. You would have thought I was a man stranded at sea in a lifeboat for days the way I flagged her down. However, she was very patient with me and said, 'How can I help you, Mr. Mannix?' I look at her tray and see all the juices. *OMG, she has apple juice! That would be perfect!* So like a five-year-old asking for a juice box, I say, 'Could I have some apple juice, please?' Just as she is about to hand me this rather large cup filled to the brim with juice and ice, we hit turbulence. The cup flies out of her hand, and she yells 'Oops!' and lunges to catch it. It looks like a scene out of *The Matrix*, as everything now goes into slow motion in my mind. The cup continues its trajectory toward me with the flight attendant desperately trying to stop it midair. But the fates would not have it. The cup lands upside down smack in my lap. It is freezing cold and covers my entire crotch area. The attendant is mortified and throws her hand towel in my lap and starts to dab vigorously, exclaiming, 'I'm so sorry. I am so sorry!' I quickly respond, 'It's okay. It's okay. Really, it's okay. Please stop dabbing.'

"Thinking I still have another seven hours to go and my only change of pants is in the belly of the plane, I need to dry this out quick. I stand up and head toward the bathroom, hoping I can use the hand dryer to get the job done. Now visualize this: People have heard the commotion but don't know what happened. They see this guy with a shockingly wet crotch heading quickly toward the bathroom. And what color is apple juice? Oh yes, you guessed it. Need I explain more? So I'm only feet from the bathroom when someone

darts in. In not such a low tone, I exclaim, 'You got to be f---
ing kidding me!' Which then draws the attention of two very
well-dressed elderly ladies sitting about a foot away. They
see my juice-covered pants, raise their hands to cover their
mouths, and exclaim in not such a subtle voice, 'Oh my,
that poor man, he had an accident in his pants!' This then
draws the attention of all the people in the area who are also
taken aback by my apparent lack of bladder control. Finally,
the person comes out from the bathroom and, like a ninja,
I dart in. Mortified, I hoist my crotch up toward the dryer
to hopefully dry things out. Well, it did, but now I still have
a stain and was totally sticky from the waist down. I leave
the bathroom after about a good twenty minutes, totally
embarrassed I open the door very slowly, saying to myself,
'Please God, please don't let the passengers notice me
heading back to my seat.'

"Well, apparently while I was in there, it became the talk
of the section I was seated in, and they were all waiting to
see me emerge. As I step out, trying to look natural, when I
turn to head back to my seat, there is a sea of faces staring at
the man who had relieved himself in his pants. Talk about
the walk of shame. I look down and head to my seat, only to
hear a number of passengers mutter, 'Thank goodness he is
not sitting next to me.' Needless to say, for the next six hours
of the flight I didn't move, as I sat there in my sticky shame.

"While it wasn't funny at that moment, I can tell you later
that night at the pub with some of my colleagues, we were
laughing so hard about it we were crying. For the record, this
story was not embellished at all. I truly hope it gave you a
good laugh. And please believe me when I say you can't take
yourself too seriously. *Laugh. Life is too short.*"

Here's another good example around Sal's father and not taking yourself too seriously. "My father would always remind us to make sure that when he dies he be buried with a bottle of scotch and a good cigar. I can clearly hear him saying to me, 'Sally, when I die, I want you to make sure you put a bottle of scotch and a good cigar in my coffin. I plan on having some fun.' Well, it was 2010, and Pop passed away at the age of ninety-one. And I did just that. My brother Johnny picked up the scotch, and I picked out one of my Cohibas and placed it in his casket. It was a small service with just our family in attendance. Before the service, my two sisters and two brothers and I met with the priest to discuss some readings and prayers that would be read before Pop—in his casket with the scotch and the cigar—would leave us for good.

"My father was a very funny person. Always smiling, laughing, or telling a joke or some wisecrack that would make you laugh. Well, the priest assigned to Pop's service was not what I expected. Turns out he was Italian, ninety-one years old (just like Pop), not very big in stature, and walked with a sort of shuffle, also just like Pop. Here's the best part: I remember all of us saying, 'Doesn't he remind you of Pop? Is this a sign?' He decided he wanted to know as much about my father and us in the twenty or so minutes before the service. He asked each of us simple questions like 'What's your name,' 'Where do you live,' and 'How many children do each of you have?' Just about everything we said to him in answer to his questions, he had a wisecrack response. Just like Pop. When my brother Joey answered his question regarding how many children he had and said 'Four children,' the priest said, 'I guess you don't watch much

TV." It was something Pop would have said. It was as if he was conducting his own funeral service.

"It gets better. So we leave the priest and find our seats in the church, chuckling as we pass the open casket with the scotch, the cigar, and Pop. The priest then comes out and walks past the casket, looks in, sees Pop, the scotch, and the cigar, and his shoulders start moving up and down as he is smiling and laughing. You can't make this up. After the service was over, we all, including the priest, had a shot of scotch as we sent Pop on his way, along with smiles, laughter, and definitely not taking life or anything at that time too seriously. Just one more thing: After everyone left the building, including Pop in the casket, my brother Johnny, my sister Toni, and my cousin Frankie and I were still in the church when a very loud bolt of thunder exploded in the sky. We all laughed. It was as if Pop was saying to all of us, 'Okay now, get the hell out of here and go live your lives. And don't take life too seriously.'"

Let's shift gears and talk seriously for a moment. The power of LAUGHTER is needed now more than ever. We all know that laughter is contagious and makes you feel good. But not everyone realizes the true health benefits of this physical reaction. Our world today is more competitive and overstimulated with all forms of media and negative forces than any other time in history. Stress levels, depression, burnout, substance abuse, and divorce are at an all-time high. More children and adults are on medication and in therapy to deal with this stress than ever before. Laughter, and truly enjoying life, or even the little things, is seriously lacking. Think about it. Take just a moment; close your eyes and think hard. When was the last time you had a good laugh? How are you feeling right now? Why are you reading this book? The bottom line is, you are either looking to be more successful, happier, or trying to find a true balance in your life. Think back to when you were a child, when life was simpler; you laughed at anything that would strike you as funny.

Studies have shown that on average a child laughs three hundred times a day while an adult laughs only seventeen times or less a day. Stop right there. Why is this? The obvious answer is that as we move from childhood to adulthood, we take on more responsibility and lose sight of the need for and importance of laughter. This change that has crept up on us over time has drastically impacted us more than we realize. It has sapped our strength little by little and robbed us of a more balanced and happier life. We also most likely do not have a full picture of all the in-depth health benefits of laughter, positive thinking, and having the right attitude.

The health benefits of laughter transcend all ages and are medically proven. Studies done by the Mayo Clinic, accredited universities, and well-respected physicians have shown the staggering positive impact of laughter. So let's take just a few moments to discuss this phenomenon that might just change your life forever. Let's begin and set the stage with some facts and figures:

- Most laughter does not come from listening to jokes; it comes from spending time with family and friends.

- People tend to laugh more when in groups. People should surround themselves with others who laugh because laughter is contagious.

- Smiling is a mild, silent form of laughing and has been shown to also have major medical benefits.

- Babies start to laugh at about four months of age and have been shown to use this as a form of communication.

Okay, so get ready to have your mind blown. Here are just some of the benefits clinically proven through the power of laughter as published by the Mayo Clinic:

Mental and Emotional Health

Humor and laughter are a powerful emotional medicine that can lower stress, dissolve anger, and unite people in troubled times. Laughing at ourselves, and the situation we are in, will help reveal that small things are not the earth-shaking events they sometimes seem to be.

Enhances Mood

Studies have shown that the simple act of laughing or smiling can improve the mood and happiness levels in subjects versus other activities. Laughter has been found to have an analgesic quality that reduces even unconscious pain, causing an improvement in mood.

Dangerous Hormones

Laughter reduces at least four of the neuroendocrine hormones associated with stress: epinephrine, cortisol, dopamine, and growth hormones, some of which have been shown to have a direct link to cancer.

Immune System

Clinical studies by Dr. Lee Berk at Loma Linda University have shown that laughter strengthens the immune system by increasing infection-fighting antibodies. Even just the act of smiling has been shown to yield similar results.

Pain Reduction

Laughter allows a person to "forget" about pains such as those associated with aches and arthritis, etc.

The Heart

Laughter, along with an active sense of humor, may help protect you against a heart attack, according to a study at the University of Maryland Medical Center. The study, which is the first to indicate that laughter may help prevent heart disease, found that people with heart disease were 40 percent less likely to laugh in a variety of situations compared to people of the same age without heart disease.

Brain Function

Laughter stimulates both sides of the brain to enhance learning. It eases muscle tension and psychological stress, which keeps the brain alert and allows people to retain more information.

Improves Memory

Along with the improved brain function that laughter can provide, it can also work to improve memory in a different way. The connections and associations that the brain forms while learning can be widened and made more complex by combining basic learning with an emotional response like laughter or humor.

Here is the one that truly blew our minds and spoke to us on a personal level.

Prevents Cancer

Laughter has also been shown to fight against cancer by increasing the levels of interferon gamma (IFN) in the body. IFN stimulates the B-cells, T-cells, NK cells, immunoglobulin, and it also works to regulate cell growth. These compounds are integral to a healthy immune system, but they are also the lines of defense against cancer and the abnormal growth of dangerous tumors in the body.

If these facts and figures don't give you an aha moment and change how you look at the importance of laughter and the power of positive thinking, we're not quite sure what will.

The bottom line: *stress kills, laughter lives.* It's that simple!

~

"Laughter is the best medicine. It can help you get through anything. Perfect example is my team. They love to laugh. We truly enjoy each other and are like a family. You spend just two minutes with them, and you better not have a drink or food in your mouth."
—Candice Corby

~

Laughter has also been shown to be a powerful tool to combat emotional distress, grief, or feelings of loss or sadness. This important key was supported during our interview with Winston Henderson: "I was at a funeral for a good friend of mine. For the service, you were supposed to wear a special tie, which I didn't have. I went to the store and bought a bunch of ties because I wasn't sure which color tie I was supposed to wear. Unbeknownst to me, as soon as

I got to the funeral, they immediately brought my friends and me to the front of the church to stand by the casket as pallbearers. So I didn't have time to put my Macy's bag down. I tucked it quickly under my arm to hide it. However, in the midst my tremendous grief, and standing in front of his entire family, this plastic bag fell out from under my arm and hit the floor. It made this very loud smack and more noise than I was comfortable having happen in this kind of grief moment. Immediately, one of my best friends, who was standing in front of me, started to awkwardly chuckle, which now, of course, made me mad, as I was fighting not to chuckle as well. Soon there were five guys, pallbearers to one of our best friends from college, who were all fighting our strong feeling of loss desperately trying to stifle this chuckle. We knew our friend was looking down and laughing at us. What this did was give us the ability to deal with this incredible level of grief that wasn't disrespectful to the family. The role of laughter was a counteragent to the grief and pain that we were all feeling.

"To this day, when we get together as a group in memory of our dear departed friend to celebrate his life, we all, including his wife, laugh so hard about my Macy's bag incident and how we knew he was laughing with us. Laughter can give you the distance to analyze some things in your life that otherwise your brain and your heart just couldn't handle."

~

There is also a very real medical detriment to not having enough laughter in your life. Let's take what happened to Mike not too long ago that shows the negative physical impact of taking yourself and life way too seriously. "On a 108-degree Thursday afternoon in New York City, I was rushing to one of my client's, stressed out as usual. I ran down to the subway platform and was waiting for the train, freaking out, as I was late for a very important meeting. The humidity on the subway platform was so thick you could almost see it, and the smell was horrific. While pacing back and forth waiting for the train that was late, I suddenly got a shooting pain down my left arm that felt like lightning. My heart began to pound out of my chest, I started to get lightheaded, the room began to spin like you see in the movies, and I passed out and hit the ground. Now, if you have ever been in a NYC subway, the last place you want to end up on the floor is on a subway platform in the middle of summer. There are all sorts of unidentified nasty things, mystery moisture, and wildlife running around. So at thirty-seven, I was rushed into the Critical Care Unit of a hospital emergency room with what I thought was a heart attack, and the nurses and doctors immediately jumped on me and began working to keep me alive. They quickly ripped off my shirt and started to run IVs and hook me up to a heart monitor. I was terrified, as I thought, *I am way too young to die; I can't go like this*, and tears started to fill my eyes. All I could think about were my children's innocent, little faces with their big brown eyes looking up at me with tears streaming down their cheeks. They were counting on me for everything, and I was now facing my mortality. I started praying silently over and over, *Please God, don't take me now; Michael and Sarah need me. Please, please God, don't take me now.* After spending what was by far one of the scariest nights of my life getting ready to be hit with paddles to restart my heart, they finally got my heart under control.

"I then spent almost a full week having more tests done than I would like to admit and being poked and prodded in places that I don't ever want to remember. Later in the week the lead doctor came into my room. I was still hooked up to IVs and the heart monitor. With my results in his hand, he sat at the edge of the bed and said, 'Let me start by saying you are *much* too young to be here; you realize that, right?' I looked at him and shook my head yes. By the way, I had my work phone in my hand and was answering emails while he was talking to me. Yes, laying in a hospital bed I was still working. Talk about workaholic and totally not getting it! He grabbed the phone out of my hand, slammed it down on the table, and said with a stern tone in his voice, 'Well, we have good news and bad news. The good news is you didn't have a heart attack but a heart event. What this means is there was no damage done to the heart, and you got off lucky. You went into what is called atrial fibrillation, better known as A-fib. The other piece of good news is that we found out what triggered the event. So now here is the bad news: You have five ulcers, one of them being esophageal, which could turn cancerous.' He then stood up and, standing with his arms crossed, disapprovingly stated, 'You need to change your life quickly, Mr. Mannix! You better get your act together and change the way you deal with stress ASAP.' He turned and walked out abruptly.

"Yes! You heard it correctly. *Five. Yes, five ulcers.* I was taking myself, my job, life, and all the pressure way too seriously. I obviously had very little self-LOVE, hardly any LAUGHTER, no LEISURE at all, and I didn't know how to LEAVE the pressure. I was all about LABOR. Bottom line:

Everything I was working so hard for could have all been lost because I was internalizing everything and not taking the time to laugh and enjoy life. So my advice is that you need to stay focused on your **5Ls** balance and make sure to LAUGH! I only wish I knew about the **5Ls** back then. Please learn from my mistakes. *Don't be a Mike Mannix.*"

~

As retired US Army Three-Star General Sean MacFarland said during our interview, "You can take your work seriously, but don't take yourself too seriously. You need to find joy in what you do. If you don't, you need to leave."

~

A lot of people will ask us what they should do if they are too stressed to laugh. What we have learned in our research is that laughter will help to change your physical and mental well-being. It brings to mind a scene from the 1987 movie *Moonstruck*, starring Cher and Nicolas Cage. There is a scene toward the end of the movie where the grandfather said during a very intense and awkward moment at the breakfast table, "Someone tell a joke!"

To be truly balanced, you must have LAUGHTER and a positive attitude in every aspect of your life. Let's take a look at your day. Your alarm went off, you got ready for work, you commuted to work or logged in from home, you worked all day and went home or shut off your computer. How many times did you laugh? Once, twice? Did you laugh at all? There are very few things in life that you have control over. One of the main things is the way you respond to something. You have the ability to choose your mood.

Mike always thought this was easier said than done. He would constantly think, *How can I choose my mood when I have so much 'crap'* (I could use stronger words) *going on in my life and coming at me?* "I felt this way for years, letting my job, circumstances, and people affect me. I had many highs and lows. I found myself mumbling under my breath, 'I hate my life.' It was like Tourette's. It would just come out; I couldn't control it. I remember saying to myself, *Mike, this is no way to live.* I felt depressed and thought I would need to go on medication—until one day when I was thinking long and hard about the 5Ls and my need for true work-life balance.

"True story: I was walking to my job in NYC, and I was just miserable once again. I was ruminating about how bad things were and was having a full on pity party. Then, like a bolt of lightning, it hit me. I stopped in the middle of a very crowded NYC sidewalk and shouted, 'Enough!' I'm sure I looked nuts to the people passing by. 'I have so much to be grateful for. So much! I'm done feeling like this! I will control the controllable; the rest is in God's hands. I'm going to choose my attitude. I am going to focus on the good things in my life.' It was like God heard my prayers. I felt this giant weight come off my chest. I could breathe again. It was unreal. I realized that staying focused on what I was grateful for and finding laughter in the day and *not* taking life and myself too seriously was the key. This has totally changed my life. We call this having an 'Attitude of Gratitude.'"

You will see throughout the book that we will back everything up with scientific data and provide you with real tools that you can implement immediately.

Let's talk about the hard science behind an Attitude of

Gratitude. In a Harvard study, it was scientifically proven that if you focus on just three things you are truly grateful for, and feel the gratitude, it will change your mental state. When you practice gratitude, a neurotransmitter called oxytocin is released in the brain. Oxytocin has taken on the nickname the "happy hormone," or the "love drug." The reason for that is because it is the same hormone that is released when you are hugging someone, making love, or deeply feeling love.

Sometimes we might need help in conjuring up these thoughts of gratitude. Here is one way that has worked for Mike. "As humans, we are very tactile creatures and need reminders in our lives. Holding or touching something can evoke a memory or feeling. After my epiphany of how having an Attitude of Gratitude could change my life, every day I started carrying in my pocket two small white stones. I call them 'Gratitude Stones.' I didn't buy them in a store or order them on Amazon. Actually, I didn't spend any money on them at all, and they are nothing special. They are just two stones that caught my eye when I was walking on my favorite beach, my happy place where I find peace. So for me, I use them as reminders of the two things in my life that I am most grateful for, my son, Michael, and my daughter, Sarah. They are truly the center of my universe. So when I am having a bad day—and I have them more than I would like—I take the stones out, hold them in my hand, close my eyes and focus on my kids. I take a few slow deep breaths and clear my mind. I think about how well they are doing, the amazing relationship I have with them, all the incredible things they are accomplishing, the beautiful young adults they are becoming both inside and out and, most of all, *how very blessed* I am to be their father. In just a few minutes, I am in a totally different headspace. This simple practice has worked miracles for me, and I teach this exercise at all of our events. I'm telling you, it works; give it a try. We all have to remember that we can only control the controllable. Choose your attitude or life will choose it for you."

Going hand in hand with having an Attitude of Gratitude is understanding and using what we call "Setting the Tone" and using the power of positive thinking in both your personal and professional life. Setting the Tone is how you approach life or respond to a situation. The way you respond to something will dictate your outcome and how others will perceive you and respond to the energy you are putting out.

Do you believe that energy is all around us? Well, it is. Think about it: Positive or negative, it surrounds us every day; in nature, in our lives, and powers the everyday tools we use. Have you ever heard the phrases, "That person just lights up the room," "They are the life of the party," or "That person has an electric personality"? This is all about energy. People that put out positive energy get positive outcomes in their life. It is the law of attraction. What you put out you get back. There have been numerous books, studies, and articles written about the power of positive thinking. Positive thinking starts with a can-do approach, as opposed to starting from a negative place. One of our clients calls this "breaking out the no": It means always start with yes.

Now, let us start out by stating that being positive is not being naïve; it's being a leader. It doesn't mean you won't have bad days; it means that you stay focused on the fact that brighter days are coming. If things don't seem to be the way you thought they were or would be does not mean you are a failure; it means there is another path or road to go down. Just because something is missing in your life, it doesn't mean it's lost forever. To quote the old Taoist proverb: "Just when the caterpillar thought the world was over, it became a butterfly."

Studies have shown that people who are positive and self-confident (and who don't take themselves too seriously) are more successful, get better jobs, attain higher output from their teams, have better relationships, and are just happier in general. As we have discussed in the LOVE chapter about self-love, self-confidence is self-love and a key trait to being a successful leader, or just successful in general. Now, we're not talking about being overconfident or coming across as arrogant (remember not to take yourself too seriously), but rather putting out positive energy and feeling good about yourself. People want to be around people that exude this trait. Think about the people you know or leaders that you admire. If they truly inspire you, they put off a positive energy that attracts you. Think about it: Do you want to be around someone that is down, ambivalent, or comes across as an emotional roller coaster? No, right? So start each day by setting a positive tone. Here is an easy mantra that you can say out loud or run through your head when you first wake up. *You fill in the blank.*

Today I will focus on...

Today I am grateful for...

Today I will let go of...

This simple practice has helped countless individuals as well as Mike personally.

In our combined seventy-plus years of business, we

have hired hundreds of people. We will tell you straight out, we will hire a person with a positive attitude who exudes positive energy every day of the week over someone who might be more qualified. Ninety percent of success is attitude, 10 percent is skill. You can teach skill; you can't teach attitude.

~

This was summed up perfectly in our interview with Sam Bei, a successful entrepreneur and restauranter. As Sammy says, "Success is all in your mind. I was being recruited for a major league team, the St. Louis Cardinals. I went to training camp, and all these guys were bigger and faster than me. I defeated myself in my mind even before I started, as I thought, *I don't belong here. I can't compete with these guys.* I thought of all the reasons why I couldn't succeed. After the first week, the coach came up to me and said, 'Are you Sam Bei? I heard you were the guy that could do all these things on the field and better than the rest. A truly gifted ballplayer. Where is that guy? If I don't see that guy show up soon, I'm sending you home.'"

As Sammy said, "I defeated myself before I even tried. That was the best thing that could have been said to me. Talk about a reality check! I put aside my doubt, took hold of a positive attitude, and really showed him what I could do. The rest is history.

"I remembered how my family was always very positive; they didn't focus on the problem, only the solution. That is why I am the way I am now. I don't let things rattle me; it is the reason for my success."

~

Just like the act of laughing, having a positive state of mind and outlook has tremendous health benefits. In a Johns Hopkins study, they were able to show that people who have a history of heart disease in their family were a third less likely to have a heart attack if they were positive individuals. Another study done by the Proceedings of the National Academy of Sciences (PNAS) showed that people who constantly maintained a positive outlook lived 15 percent longer than individuals that had a consistent negative attitude.

On the flip side of the coin, the University College of London showed in a recent study that people who stayed in a negative attitude state for long periods of time started to exhibit the same biomarkers in the brain as someone with Alzheimer's. We don't know about you, but that scared the hell out of us.

Setting the proper tone and utilizing a positive attitude all starts with positive communication. Understanding how people process information is critical. You need to keep in mind that people's perception is their reality. To be truly successful, you need to understand how individuals actually process what you are saying and how you are coming across. This is imperative to understand and master both in your personal and professional life in order to be successfully balanced. So if your words, tone, and how you come across is negative, you will be perceived as negative, and people will respond to you accordingly.

Now let's take a deeper dive at how people process information. If you break communication down into its most basic components and the way people process information, it falls into three categories, which is defined in what is called the Communication Pyramid. The pyramid is broken down into three key components:

- **Words**: What you are actually saying.
- **Tone and Inflection**: How you are saying it and the inflection in your voice.
- **Body Language**: How you physically carry yourself—the way you stand, move, sit, facial expressions, etc.

If you break these down by percentage to equal 100 percent, how do you think they would break out? What percent do you think each component equals? Take a second before you read further. In your mind, have a percentage for each component. Once you have these percentages fixed in your mind then get ready to be quite surprised.

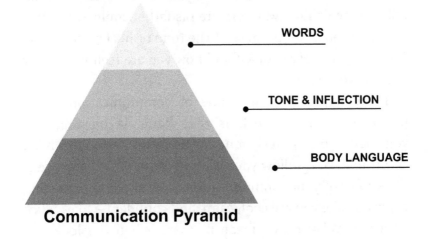

Communication Pyramid

Ready to have your mind blown once more? Here is how it breaks out. This is how people process your conversation.

- **Words**: 7 percent.
- **Tone and Inflection**: 38 percent.
- **Body Language**: 55 percent.

This should be a real eye opener for you and, frankly, scare you a little. What you are actually saying, the words coming out of your mouth, carries the least impact in the way people process information. How you actually say the words is next. The way you carry yourself has the most impact on any communication and the way you are perceived. Body language also impacts communication even when you are not in front of someone. For example, do you think you can hear a smile? Well, the answer is yes, you can. As Sal would tell you, he could always picture his father smile every time they were on a call because of the tone of his father's voice. The way you carry yourself and how you are feeling actually impacts your tone.

Therefore, if your first line of communication, be it personal or professional, is that Rome is burning and your hair is on fire, everyone in the room is going to react accordingly and follow your lead. Because body language is 55 percent of your communication, how about approaching every day like you are cool, calm, and confident—like a *duck on water*. What do we mean by that? When you look at a duck in a pond, they look like they are gliding effortlessly. What you don't see is that under the surface their feet are paddling like crazy. So if you are going to set a positive tone, no matter how stressed out you are, keep it under the surface. The type of person that people want to be around or follow make it look easy; they aren't emotional roller coasters or show the stress or pressure they are under. Remember, you set the tone.

What stress management tools do you have in place to give you the ability to stay positive? We will talk more about this in the LEISURE chapter, but without these tools you will crash and burn. Things like exercise, meditation, journaling, breathing techniques, and finding your Me Time are just a few; you need to find what works best for you. Also, using an Attitude of Gratitude and choosing your attitude like we discussed in LOVE are incredibly effective. What you will also notice is that there are tools in every one of the 5Ls that will give you the ability to navigate stress, anxiety, and depression that will apply to and impact every aspect of your life, be it personal or professional.

In your professional life, whether you are in management or not, your team responds to the energy you are putting out. Positive is good, negative is not. If you are negative, that translates to your team. If you are putting out positive energy, that also transfers to your team and their performance. Laughter is contagious. If you set the tone for a creative, positive, and safe atmosphere, you will see the results. We have done this for all our teams, and this has translated into them not only meeting but constantly exceeding their goals.

~

During our interview with Regina Bei, a successful restaurateur and entrepreneur, she felt that humor and a positive attitude were the most important aspects in motivating, retaining your team, and being a good leader. "A good manager needs to be positive and focused on making a conscious effort to be funny."

~

But let's stay with communication for a moment, as this impacts every aspect of your life. There are four key components to communication you need to keep top of mind: First, you should be *authentic*. This is critical. If people think you are being fake you will never gain their trust. Second, be *direct*. Don't beat around the bush. Say what you mean with respect for the other person, and they will perceive you as honest and not wishy-washy. Third, be *succinct*. We discussed that people only hear about 7 percent of what you are saying. Here is another piece of news: People don't read. That is why text messaging is so popular. People want it short and sweet. Think about it: Have you ever gotten a super long email? If you are being honest, you might have skimmed it for the key points, right? Finally, be *present*. Be in the now and actively listen. This shows the person that you care and that what they're telling you is important.

Here is a question for you: Do you think you are a good multitasker? If the answer is yes, we have some bad news for you. There is no such thing. Multitasking is doing more than one thing at the same time poorly. So if you are texting or typing an email while you are speaking to someone, *stop it!* We just told you that you are only grasping about 7 percent *if* you are actually listening. What do you think you're getting if you are only partially paying attention? Here is the worst part: You are telling the person that is trying to tell you something—potentially very important—that you just don't care and they are not as important as what you are doing.

One more point: You can never *overcommunicate*. A vacuum will create dissent and fear. Better to keep people in the know, because if you don't, they will come up with their own perception of reality, and it will usually be negative.

Let's talk about that for a second. *People's perception is their reality*. Whether it is the truth or not, it is their reality. People, without thinking, will judge a situation even before they get to it. Usually, it's negative first. Think about it: Why is the news negative almost all the time? It's because they know it sells ratings. Well, why is that? The reason, and what you might not know, is going back to prehistoric times, as humans we are preprogrammed to go to the negative first. This was to make you approach every situation with caution so you didn't get eaten. This is also why some people find it so hard to be positive. But here is the good news: There is such a thing as neuroplasticity. That means that no matter how old you are, you can retrain your mind and learn something new. So now that you know this, you can stop beating yourself up for thinking in a negative way, and change it. Remember, control the controllable. And the one thing you can control is how you respond and the energy you put out.

Staying positive is also impacted by outside negativity. We highly recommend limiting your *news and social media intake*. The news is predominantly negative, as discussed, to sell ratings. Social media is usually someone's highlight reel and a total misrepresentation of reality. Have you ever seen someone post "I suck" or "My kids suck"? No. It's usually, "Look how fantastic my life is!" What message this sends out is that if your life is not as good as theirs, you are a failure or less than. It's not real, and unfortunately, people are measuring themselves against it. This is *impacting mental health and is a real problem.*

The detrimental health impact of constant negative information intake and the effects of social media on children has been clinically documented. The Harvard School of Public Health stated, "We've known for years that social media platforms, especially image-based platforms, have very harmful effects on teen mental health, especially for teens struggling with body image, anxiety, depression, and eating disorders." We highly recommend making sure you and your family limit this type of exposure as much as possible.

Now that we just took a deep dive into the power of positive thinking and communication, here are just a few stats on the effect of how humor and positive thinking impacts your career and the ability to lead and grow, as stated by the *Harvard Business Review*:

- **Humor enhances perceived leadership skills.** "People who use humor, particularly in stressful situations, are viewed as being on top of things, being in charge and in control, whether they are in fact or not."

- **Humor creates more opportunities.** "Research has shown that managers displaying a good sense of humor are given more opportunities in organizations than those without a sense of humor."

- **Humor builds credibility.** "Humor users are seen as more credible and as more competent."

- **Humor increases size of paycheck.** "The size of their bonuses correlated positively with their use of humor."

- **Humor increases profit.** "Organizational humor has been linked with successful leadership, with increases in profit and work compliance."

The atmosphere you create will also impact your team around you in a positive or negative manor. In numerous studies, it has been shown that being positive and utilizing humor in the workplace improves motivation, reduces absenteeism, prevents long-term burnout, improves productivity, and increases overall employee retention and engagement.

~

This was summed up perfectly in another story from our interview with retired major leaguer Tommy John: "To me, the best managers I had were the ones that made the game fun. Tommy Lasorda was the best. You would go through hell in a gasoline suit for Tommy. He made it fun! I would do anything for him. I would do whatever I could do to help the Dodgers win when Tommy was there. He might not have been a good manager in Xs and Os, but the guys would give 120 percent because he believed in us and made the game fun!"

~

Some people are funny, and they don't even know it. Take Rande Bynum, who told us, "I think I am funny, but I have recently learned that maybe I'm not. That in itself is funny. One of the eight-year-old Girl Scouts introduced me to another Girl Scout and said, 'This is Rande. You will get used to her, with her jokes and stuff.' I guess I tell bad jokes, and I find myself laughing and no one else is laughing. Apparently, the lack of humor that I have is funny to others, which is an icebreaker and makes people feel at ease. I think you have to just giggle at some stuff, even if people are laughing at you. It can be engaging, and you tend to come across as approachable. Apparently, I'm not that funny."

~

So let's bring the laughter back into your life. It will improve your mental and physical well-being, your relationships, your career, your success, and your overall quality of life.

When Bob Newhart was asked "How has your marriage lasted fifty-seven years," he said without hesitation, "Laughter!"

~

As Rande Bynum stated, "LAUGHTER speaks to me the most. The best moments and strongest of my life, even if it's just my mom and me at the kitchen table, involve laughing. As an adult, being able to have the gut-wrenching laugh is crucial and the moments I treasure most. Not to mention, put you in a better state of mind."

~

It is so simple. We knew it as children. *So laugh*! Bring the laughter and the power of positive thinking back into your life. It might just change your world.

One last story from Mike to end the chapter. When you first start to read this story, you are most likely going to say to yourself, *Why the heck is this in the LAUGHTER chapter?*

Just give it to the end, and I promise it will make sense.

"In the final days before my father lost his battle with cancer, he had one last request: He didn't want to die in hospice. He wanted to be home in his bed in the house we all grew up in and that he worked so hard to provide for us. Of course, we honored this and transported him home. We all made the collective decision to stay at the house to make sure we were there when the time finally came. I stayed in my old room with my kids; my sister Jen, her husband, and my niece in hers; and my sister Rosemarie stayed in hers. It was surreal for us to all be home again, but it just felt right. We were there for a week when I needed to head back to my house to pick up more clothes for my kids and me. I live about an hour away from my parents' house.

"I remember that night like it was yesterday. I was up in my daughter's room packing the bag when my phone rang. I looked at the screen; it was my mother. This sick feeling came over me. First thought was, *Oh my God, my father passed, and I missed being there for him.* I answered the phone, 'Mom, is everything okay?' My mother was hysterically crying. Through her tears she responded, 'Michael, we are losing him. You need to come now!' I didn't even respond. I dropped everything I was doing, ran downstairs and out the front door. I don't remember if I left the front door wide open or not; I just bolted. I flew into my car and peeled out of the driveway. I drove like a maniac from my house to the Long Island Expressway (LIE), breaking every speed limit and blowing stoplights. I got on the LIE and slammed my foot on the gas. The engine roared, and I took off like a shot. I must have averaged a hundred miles an hour all the way out to my parents' exit. While in transit, I think I called my mother fifteen times to tell her where I was and to please tell dad I was almost there. I have no idea how I didn't get pulled over.

"While breaking land speed records to get to my father, I remember how dark the night was. It was an eerie black that just made your skin crawl. The moon, however, was full and enormous. It literally filled the sky and lit the road. I loudly prayed most of the way out, 'God, please don't take him yet. Please let me get to him in time.' It became almost like a mantra, as I said it over and over again till I got off at my parents' exit. I called my mother for the final time: 'Mom, I'm off the exit.' She put her phone on speaker and put it next to my father. Trying to keep calm, I said, 'Dad, I am almost there. I'm almost there.' My mother hung up, and I proceeded to drive to my parents' house like a professional stunt man.

"I made it to my parents' home and screeched into the driveway. With the car still running, I leaped from the driver's seat and left the door wide open. I hit the back door, raced through the house and up the stairs to my parents' room. As I got to the doorway, I heard my mother say, 'He made it, Mike. It's okay; he is here now.' My sisters and my mother were all around him. I sat on the bed, grabbed his hand in mine and said, 'I'm here, Dad. We are all here. You have been the best father that we could ever have asked for. You have given us so much, and we are all in good places. We will be okay. I promise we will be okay; you can go now.' With that, my father's breath started to labor, his chest going up and down slowly. My sisters and my mother were sobbing softly. I felt my father's grip start to loosen. His breath became slower, and I also started to sob. Just then, my father, who had lost the power of speech a few days before, opened his eyes wide, smiled, shook his head and said, 'Nope, not yet,' and started to softly laugh. I looked at him in shock and said, 'What the (four letter word), Dad; what did you just say?' With a big smile, he shook his head no, as in 'Not my time yet, folks,' and continued to chuckle. Once we all realized how funny my father thought this whole thing was, we all started to laugh while wiping our eyes. Talk about a drama-filled situation! And my dad being my dad, realizing it wasn't his time yet, showed us once again the power and need for LOVE and LAUGHTER.

"One of the things my family has always shared is how we make each other laugh. All our holidays and times together were filled with us teasing each other relentlessly and laughing so hard our sides would hurt. There was no way you could take yourself too seriously at the Mannix's. We would always say we put the *fun* in *dysfunctional*. Right to the end, my father was teaching us how very important it is to love each other, not to take yourself too seriously, and to make sure to always laugh."

As we did in the LOVE section, take a quick second to think of the color that comes to mind when you hear the word *Laughter*. Remember that for the end of the book.

~

Once again here is our **5Ls** Self-Assessment Tool. Answer yes or no to these ten simple questions as honestly as you can. If the question is something you are on the fence about or have just somewhat in your life, then the answer should be "No." If you have less than seven "Yes" answers, that is an indicator that you need to work on this particular "L" to find your **5Ls** balance.

LAUGHTER

"Y"	"N"	
		Do I know not to take myself and life too seriously?
		Do I realize that my mistakes are my best teacher?
		Do I practice daily the power of positive thinking?
		Do I realize that laughter is one of the best forms of therapy?
		Do I limit the news and social media to watch something that makes me laugh?
		Do I laugh more than I stress?
		Do I laugh more than 17 times a day?
		Do I look for opportunity in a bad situation?
		Do I use laughter to help with stress and depression?
		Do I seek out people and things that bring laughter and joy to me?

CHAPTER THREE

—

LABOR

"Nothing will work unless you do."
—Maya Angelou

As human beings, *we are built to work, wired to produce,* and have an inherent desire to have *passion and purpose* in what we do. When we say this, we are not just talking about the need to earn money for a living. We are talking about the most essential need for your well-being: *Purpose.* People at their essence need to work, or LABOR on, something to give them passion and purpose. It provides a sense of usefulness and belonging as well as providing financial means. It gives us a sense of self-worth and a sense of contributing to society for the common good. Without meaningful work in our life, we degenerate.

An object in motion stays in motion. You might not realize it, but labor gives us multiple benefits. Through your labor you will leave a legacy. Labor gives our lives meaning, makes us feel useful, and keeps our minds sharp. It also supports personal and social identity, physical and mental well-being, and self-confidence. Oh yes, it does help pay the bills.

What is the first image that comes to mind when you hear the word *labor*? Don't think; just hear the word *labor*. What is the first thing that comes to you? Is it positive or negative? We can guarantee 98 percent of the time that you will visualize something negative. Why is that? Well, it's pretty much because the majority of society looks at it this way. Just look up the definition of labor: "work, especially hard physical work." Synonyms: work, hard work, toil, exertion, industry, drudgery, effort, menial work. Okay, so therein lies the problem. That mindset is all wrong.

If you want to lead a truly happy, well balanced, and successful life, you need to flip that perspective now. Let's take a step back and think about this at the core.

Numerous studies have shown some pretty scary negative effects after retirement. What is being seen is that if someone no longer has purpose in their life once they retire, within one year their health declines rapidly, sometimes leading to death. A recent study done by the National Bureau of Economic Research concluded that complete retirement leads to a 5–16 percent increase in difficulties associated with mobility and daily activities, a 5–6 percent increase in illness conditions, and 6–9 percent decline in mental health.

As Mike will tell you, his father in-law—God rest his soul—was eighty-five years old and still got up and traveled into the office every day. From a financial perspective, he didn't need to work. He truly loved what he did, and by all means it kept him going in many ways. "My wife and I talked about it all the time that his job is what kept him so sharp and vibrant for so long. If we are being truly honest with ourselves, it is what's kept him alive till eighty-five and able to beat cancer three times. It kept him challenged, his mind working, and he felt appreciated and respected. It gave him purpose."

These are some of the most basic needs for humans. Stay on that for a second. Isn't that what we all really want, to be accepted, respected, and appreciated? Meaningful labor gives us these much-desired basic needs. It really is some of the best medicine. So you need to erase that old perspective and reprogram your thinking when you hear the word LABOR.

To be successful, however, you need to do more than just work at a job; you need to find what you are deeply passionate about. This is the key. Take a moment and think about this: What are you passionate about? What are you good at? What have others told you you're good at?

～

This was another great point that came out of our interview with Ollie Crom: "Successful is doing that what you love to do. Forget about how much money you might make; you will be successful if you follow your dream. If you go to work because you can get more money there, you might be miserable; most people are."

～

Has anyone ever said to you, "Wow, you really missed your calling in life; you are so good at this"? The common mistake is, this is seen as telling someone, "Hey, great job!" And maybe it is meant that way. Mike had this said to him on a regular basis, and he did not see it as a positive. This is how he looked at it: "I have to tell you, one of the things that I was struggling with every day is, I had not found my calling, or my passion. I was just working like crazy to pay the bills. However, from time to time for my job I would do a presentation, a keynote speech, teach a class, or act as the master of ceremonies for the company's holiday event. I loved every minute of doing those things, and it showed. It never failed; someone would always come up to me right after and say, 'Wow, Mike, that was great! You really missed your calling.' While I would smile and say thank you, I was totally pissed off. Not at the person saying it, but at myself, as it was yet another reminder that I wasn't doing what I was born to do. To me, that meant I missed what I was supposed to be doing in life, my purpose. That was just sickening. I would think, *I missed it. It's gone. Really?! What the hell. I really need to get this figured out fast!* It upset me to my core every time because I was not doing what I was passionate about. While I had a good job that I'm sure a lot of people would give their left arm for, it wasn't my calling. I wanted to be doing something that helped motivate, inspire, develop, and change people's lives for the better. Have you ever just known down deep inside that you were wasting every day but making excuses on why you needed to stay? I have to tell you, this ate at my very being for years. I needed to use all 5Ls to finally make the change to where I am today. It took me way too long before I figured it out. Don't let this happen to you. It is critical to have passion and purpose for what you do in your life. Period. It truly is that important."

~

A great example of this is from our interview with General Sean MacFarland, "To be successful, you have to measure yourself against both internal and external criteria. You need to set a goal for your life and pursue it. Internally, your goal doesn't need to be like anyone else's. It has to be what gets you out of bed in the morning, your passion and purpose. Externally, others have to benefit from your existence, how you made the human race better."

~

So why wasn't Mike doing what he wanted to do? He needed that job to pay the bills and maintain his lifestyle. Does this sound familiar? Have you ever heard the term "Golden Handcuffs"? There is not a more accurate visual. They truly are handcuffs that keep you captive, keep you down, and keep you from fulfilling what you are truly meant to do. You were not meant to be mediocre! You were meant for so much more. Reality is, if you want to be truly successful, you need to have love or passion for what you labor at. If you are not passionate about what you do, you can never be truly successful. You will wake up every day demotivated, unfulfilled, and dreading every Monday. You will have that crowded NYC sidewalk moment when you cry out, "I can't do this anymore!" like Mike mentioned in LAUGHTER.

Here is something else Mike would tell you: "I would get what I like to call the 'Sunday night blues.' Like clockwork, at 5:00 p.m. every Sunday evening, my mood would change. No matter what I was doing I would start to get down and obsess on what I must accomplish over the next week. This is truly not the way to live.

"There is no greater waste than burying your talent. Bottom line: If you bury your talent in a job that you do not have passion for, you will never grow and never reach your full potential. For many years, I buried my talents, and not only didn't reach my full potential, but I was unfulfilled. It took me more time than I would like to admit to finally get out of the Golden Handcuffs. I did this by stopping the excuses. On the side, I started working with Sal on this book and with Unparalleled Performance until the time was right to LEAVE. I will go deeper into that when we get to that chapter.

"What I am doing today is truly my calling and what I believe I was born to do. It was a huge risk—and I can't say I wasn't scared—but it has been worth every minute. When starting on something new like this you need to stay positive. LAUGHTER and the power of positive thinking is key. I tell my children and my students, 'Do what you love and the money will follow.' *What is critical to understand and what you will see about every "L," it all ties back to self-love. There is a reason LOVE is the first "L." All roads lead to love.* When you are truly passionate about what you do, it shows. You can't help but see when someone really loves what they do. By exuding this passion, you will get recognized, and you will be successful."

Life in general is all about the standard you set for yourself. This is certainly true in what you choose to work at or LABOR on. You will only achieve the standard you set— what you are willing to tolerate in your life and nothing less. If you set your standard low, that is what you will achieve. If you set your standard high, you will not settle for anything less than that, and you will achieve it! Better to set your standard high and miss than set your standard low and hit it.

Have you ever heard the term "labor of love"? Have you ever been up all night working on something that is your calling and felt totally energized the next day? Well, that is the key to success. You need to find your passion, your calling, and pursue it. When you are doing what you love, you function at a completely different level. Your energy, drive, and creativity are on high. This combination will take your productivity to an unmatched peak. Wouldn't it be great to look forward to Monday and not have the anxiety start creeping in around 4:00 or 5:00 p.m. on Sunday?

If you can't for some reason do what you are passionate about for a living at this moment in time, then you need to find something you love outside of work and LABOR at it. You need this as your fuel to keep you going. You need this to keep you motivated and your energy/mental state positive until you can get to your dream job. This impacts every aspect of your life. How many people come home from a hard day at work and take it out on the ones they love? LABOR is now crossing over and impacting LOVE. You see how the 5Ls continue to overlap? If it doesn't impact the ones around you, it just keeps eating away at you until you become depressed. Eventually this can negatively affect your health and performance, thus impacting self-love or pushing you to leave, potentially not on your own accord.

It is so key to have passion and love for what you do to be successful. If you can't leave your job and can't do something outside of the job for *you*, then find what you love in your current role and focus on it.

~

One last story on this line of thought. During our interview with Winston Henderson, he described how his father found his true passion and purpose after retirement.

"My father was a probation and corrections officer for many years. After some time in the service, he came to Brooklyn where he became a teacher. When he retired, he moved back to that same small town in South Carolina in his sixties and realized that just like when he left, there was no school. The elementary school students and middle school students would have to travel over an hour to get to the closest school. My father knew this needed to change. So my father, who was supposedly retired, ran for mayor, and won. Once he took office, he then raised state and federal funds and built a school for the children. After leaving this town forty years prior, his passion and purpose created the change that was so desperately needed."

~

Now let's talk about LABOR in a different context: Relationships—the need to find time to work on the important relationships in your life. A truly healthy relationship takes work; it doesn't just happen. If you don't realize this, you will be one very lonely individual. You need to be there for your loved ones. Sal tells this story straight from the heart on the detrimental effect of only having one "L" dominate your life.

"Years ago, I was vice-chairman of a multibillion-dollar global marketing communications company, operating in over 130 countries. My life was my work—which I admit was a mistake. Over 50 percent of my life was traveling the globe. I used to measure my business trips not by the cities I visited but by the countries I visited. I was so wrapped up in my work I did not even realize that my marriage was falling apart or that I was really an absentee dad."

I certainly didn't have my **5Ls** in any balanced way. And again, I created them. I didn't have LOVE, in my life—certainly not self-love. LAUGHTER, forget about it; I was taking myself way too seriously. LABOR, well, yes and no. I had too much labor, as I let my job define me. No way was I working on the important relationships in my life. LEISURE, I barely took any time off. And as for LEAVE, I didn't know when to pivot and move on.

We will talk about this later in the chapter about having only one of the **5Ls** in your life and not the balance of all of them and the negative impact that can have on your life.

"When you fail to labor on the important relationships in your life, you will fail. My idea of being a meaningful, loving father and the relationship with my son, Matthew, was a daily phone call. I look back and think, *Sal, how did you not see this is as a recipe for failure? You're a smart person. Come on. Seriously; it wasn't that complicated.* But I was blinded by my obsession with my work and the strong desire to be successful. I did not have a very good perspective on what was needed to show that my relationship with my family was the most important thing in my life. I lost my **5Ls** balance, and I was the person that created them.

"I wasn't working on the most important relationships in my life. It was a mistake, and it was costly. My idea of working on my relationship was when I was traveling I never changed my watch to the time of the country I was visiting. I did that so I would always be on NY time; I wanted to be able to call Matthew every day at 7:30 a.m. NY time. I did this every day, as it was just before he would be leaving for school at St. Roberts Grammar School in Bayside, New York. It didn't matter where I was in the world or what I was doing; when my watch read 7:30 NY time, I would excuse myself from whomever I was meeting with—or even set an alarm if I was sleeping (because of the time difference)—to make that call. The time difference could be six or sixteen hours, but I never missed it. The call was usually about three minutes and went something like this: Susan, my ex-wife, would answer the phone. I'd say, 'Good morning, Sue. Is Matt there?' She would say, 'Hold on.' And I could hear her saying, 'Matt, it's your father.' Matt would pick up the phone, and I would say, 'Hey, pal. How you doing?' He would say, 'Okay.' I would then say, 'You getting ready for school?' He would say, 'Yeah.' I would say, 'Okay. Have a good day,' and end with 'love you.' He would then end on his side by saying, 'love you too.' And that was it. I didn't even say the words 'I love you'; it was just 'love you,' every day without fail. And this was what I thought was good enough. This is what I thought I had to do, which led to my failed way of having a meaningful relationship with my son. Seriously, I look back and say, *Sal, how could you think you were working on the most important relationships in your life?* Damn! What was I thinking?

"That was what I used to think was good enough—to let him know that even though I was never around, I loved him so much that I would call him every day no matter where I was. Well, it wasn't enough. That doesn't work in any acceptable way to maintain and grow a most-important relationship and, in this case, my son. It took me using all the **5Ls** and nearly fifteen years of truly working on (or laboring on) this to get to a loving and wonderful relationship. Now not a day goes by that I don't talk to Matthew, and that means the world to me.

"That epiphany, the revelation that the important relationships in your life need to be labored on has brought more joy in my life than I could ever dream of. I now enjoy an irreplaceable relationship with my son and his beautiful family.

"So here are some pearls of wisdom from my beautiful granddaughter Giuliana, so smart and so wise at such a young age. Several years ago, when she was about three years old, she was working on a puzzle. I was impressed with her ability to solve it so quickly. It seemed pretty difficult to me. I tried several times to solve it, without success. Finally, 'G,' as I call her, looked at me and said, 'Grandpa, do like me do,' as she slowly walked me through her successful solving of the puzzle. I heeded her advice and did exactly like she showed me, and I solved the puzzle.

"I say to you all, as it relates to the important relationships in your life, sometimes you need to work at them more than you realize, keeping them healthy and loving. As my granddaughter said, 'Grandpa, do like me do.' I am telling you, 'Please don't do like me do.' LABOR on those important relationships in your life. Live the 5Ls balance."

Another key in any meaningful relationship is to understand that you are not always going to agree or see eye to eye. You will go through hard times. The only constant you can count on in life is change. Life will throw curveballs your way, and you need to make sure you work on these challenges in true partnership. *Compromise, communicate, show respect, be there for each other, and by all means, have each other's back!* It is the cornerstone of any true partnership. Life will come at you; it will have its ups and downs. You need to be there for and support each other. If you can't count on each other for that support, then it is not a true partnership. The grass is not always greener on the other side. Sometimes it only takes watering what you have. Not always the case but something to consider.

The same thought process needs to be applied when it comes to your friendships. At its most basic elements, to be a true friend is about a strong relationship. It takes all the same dedication and commitment we just discussed. What is critical here is investing your time and energy in the right people. You need to surround yourself with people that are *for you* no matter what, who are positive and lift you up. You need to cut the Energy Vampires out of your life that we discussed in LOVE. It goes back to standards. If you allow negative people in your life, you will become negative. If you truly want to be successful, you need to invest in the people that will raise you up, keep you motivated, and support you in good times and bad. These are called confidants. Seek them out and invest your time and energy in them! They are like diamonds: *rare and truly hard to find.*

~

This was echoed in our interview with Ollie Crom. Ollie eloquently told us, "My definition of success might be a little different than others'. I tell my children, 'If in a lifetime you have four or five truly close friends, you have lived a successful life; someone you can call at three in the morning and say, 'I have a problem,' and they will be there for you, that is true success."

~

It is also very important that you work (LABOR) on and invest in yourself. To achieve success, you need Me Time.

You will see this in LEISURE. You are no good to others if you don't take care of yourself. This goes back to what we talked about in LOVE, the Oxygen Mask Theory. You need to focus on *you*. What do you have for you that fuels you, that feeds your soul, something you are passionate about that motivates you? This is so imperative for mental and spiritual health. Unfortunately, investing in oneself is usually what people sacrifice first. "I don't have time for me; I am too busy providing." Does this sound familiar? This is a perilous error. Self-sacrifice is the opposite of self-love. Focus on you. Invest in you.

Let's take it a step further. Are you learning something new every day? Are you growing? If you are not learning, you are not growing. If you are not growing and developing, you will be left behind. In just about every interview we conducted with highly successful people for this book, the idea of self-development, or personal growth, was paramount and top of mind.

~

General MacFarland said, "Learning and growing is critical to finding balance, happiness, and success in your life." He also stated, "Learning is the key to this. It's what differentiates us as a species."

~

We could not agree more. Mike always says, "I can personally tell you, the older I get the more I realize what I don't know. I make it a point to try to learn something new every day. No matter how big or small, I have to gain something I didn't know before." So when you think of investing in yourself, these four words need to be at the forefront: *learn, grow, develop, evolve*. So if you are truly committed to this process, start with laboring on yourself every day.

~

As General David Perkins stated so well in our interview, "When you realize you have a lot to learn, every day you seek to learn more. When you think you know it all, you stop being successful."

~

Let's stay on the subject of laboring on yourself and share with you a story about Mike's son, Michael. "When my son, Michael, was born, it was one of the most magical days of my life. I was twenty-eight and had no idea how to be a dad or what to expect. I was terrified of what the future would hold and that this new-to-the-world little person would be counting on me for the rest of his life. Even with all this running through my head, I have to tell you that when the nurse handed him to me for the first time, it changed my world. I started to talk to him, saying the same words I would say at night to his mom's pregnant belly. So let me explain that for a second before you think I'm nuts.

"We were told that a baby's auditory system develops early on. That is why the baby knows its mother's voice. So I decided I wanted in on that action. Now, I'm sure if you saw it, you would have thought I was as crazy as his mom was laying in the bed that there was this soon-to-be-dad saying to her belly, 'Hey, little guy, it's your daddy. I love you so much, and I can't wait to meet you.' And, crazy or not, like clockwork, he would start to kick, and his mom and I would both get these huge smiles on our faces.

"So back to the delivery room. The moment he heard my voice, this little squishy, pink-faced baby stopped crying, turned his head, opened his eyes, and looked at me. The nurse said, 'Oh my God! He recognizes your voice! In my twenty years of being a nurse, I have never seen that; it is truly amazing.' Right then and there I was done. I fell in love with this little guy in such a way I cannot put into words.

"In the beginning, Mike was hitting all his milestones: sitting up, crawling, starting to walk, and starting to talk. However, shortly after receiving his MMR shot, he went silent and started to have sensory issues. We were so worried about what was happening to our little boy. We took him to many doctors, who all gave us different diagnoses. We finally took him to a team of doctors that worked together to come up with the final diagnosis that he had some autistic symptoms, but their final prognosis was a heavy speech delay disorder with learning differences. As you can imagine, our hearts sank, and we were devastated. We asked ourselves questions like, *What will this mean for him? What will his life be like?* You know, all the questions you would ask yourself as a worried parent. We got him services right away and did everything you can imagine to desperately help our little guy. Even with all our desperate attempts, Mike remained silent almost till the age of five.

"Let's fast forward to sixth grade. Even with his speech issues and learning differences at the time, Mike had the dream to become President of the United States—a lofty goal to say the least. He loved the idea of politics and being able to help people. He decided quickly that he wanted to run for President of the school's student government when he reached the eighth grade. Now keep in mind, we had over twelve hundred students in our junior high school. They hold a true election with vote counting, and you must give a speech to the entire student body on why you should be President of the Student Government Association (SGA) and what you are going to do for the school. Mike knew this and told me that he was going for it, and nothing was going to stop him. Please keep in mind, part of Mike's challenges was having a really hard time getting his thoughts out—and you know kids can be mean to kids that are different. I had nightmares of him having to give this type of speech in front of the entire school and the taunting that might follow. But this determined young man was not going to let this stop him. For the next two years, he worked harder than ever with his speech therapist on improving his abilities.

"When eighth grade came around, we wrote his speech together. For over two months, day and night, he would practice with me or in front of the mirror. He would stumble, pronounce words incorrectly, and forget things, but he would push through his discouragement. The night before the big day neither of us could sleep. He must have come into my room ten times throughout the night asking, 'Dad, are you up? I'm really nervous; can we talk?' He was so scared yet wanted this more than anything.

"As I am getting him and his sister ready for school the next morning, he says, 'Hey, Dad, I think I want to wear a suit to school for my big speech.' In my mind I'm thinking, *No, buddy, not a suit. The kids are going to have just another thing to make fun of.* But I responded, 'Are you sure, Mike?'

He said, 'Yup. I just need you to tie my tie for me.' Of course, the next thought for me was, *Oh no, not a tie too. The kids are going to love that.* But I did what he asked, got him dressed and him and Sarah off to school. As I turned to walk away from the school bus, I looked back and saw him in the window. He was so proud of himself; he was just beaming.

"Now, picture in your mind a huge school auditorium with over a thousand kids grades six through eight. Mike and the other candidates were sitting in chairs on the stage flanked by the Principal and the Vice Principal. The noise of the students can only be equated to that of a Super Bowl game. The Principal finally stepped up to the mic and got the students under control. He then proceeded to ask them for their attention and introduced all the candidates. Next he invited the first candidate to give their speech. One by one they got up and told of why they should be President. Some were well prepared, and some way too cool to prep and were making it up on the fly. After each one, a halfhearted round of applause was received. Finally, Mike, the only one in a suit and last to go, was announced. He confidently marched up to the podium and launched into his speech quickly, gesturing with his hands and hitting his points hard. He was flawless. Tears of pride filled my eyes as I watched him transform into this powerful orator. He was perfect, never missed a beat, and went through all the reasons why they should vote for him.

"Finally he wrapped up and finished with a strong 'Thank you! I am Mike Mannix, and I am running for your student government President!' You could hear a pin drop, and there was a pause that felt like a lifetime. Then within seconds, an explosion of applause followed by a standing ovation. His teachers were crying with pride, hugging each other over the boy who couldn't speak for the longest time and worked so hard on himself to overcome his speech challenge and had finally reached his dream of becoming President of the SGA.

"Mike is now in his twenties and continues to beat the odds. He always says to me, 'I believe we all have a purpose in life; we just need to work for it.' I could not agree more."

I'm sure you are wiping your eyes after that story, but let's turn the focus back to you and ask you a question. What are you passionate about? Now be honest with yourself on these next questions. Do you have that passion in your life? Do you work on it each and every day? Is one of these passions something that is only for you?

Here are two quick exercises that Mike learned a number of years ago that have changed his life, and we now use it in all our trainings. Here is the first one:

Get a blank piece of paper. At the top, write the number 168. Then in the left-hand column, write in descending order the numbers one through three. Make sure to leave room in between. Now take a few moments and think hard on this: List out the top three most important things in your life, and what you are passionate about. However, make sure that one of them is for you and only you. Something that doesn't involve others that develops you or pushes towards a goal. Now, once you have them, in the right-hand column write the amount of time you spend on each in a week. Be honest with yourself. Is it ten minutes, thirty minutes, a few hours, an entire day? Whatever it is, write it out.

Okay, now that you have this, do you know what the number 168 is? *It is the number of hours in a week.* So if you are not focusing some real amount of time on the top three things in your life, that is a real problem. Some people say to us, "Well, 168 includes the hours in which you sleep." Alright, fair enough. But think about this, have you ever gotten up early for work, worked late into the night for your job? Well then, how about doing that for *you*? *Make working on you first your top priority.* It's that important.

Another one of the many tools we teach in our classes for laboring on yourself is the *process of time management and prioritizing* what is important in your life. It is called the Bottle, Big Rocks, and Sand concept. Here is the premise:

- **The Bottle** = you or the amount of time you have.

- **The Big Rocks** = the truly important things in your life, what you are passionate about and will move you forward.

- **The Sand** = all the noise and/or things that fill up your day that are truly just distractions.

So the question is posed, if you need to get all the rocks and sand in the bottle, what goes in first? Answer: If you put the sand in first you will never fit all the big rocks. However, if you put the big rocks in first then add the sand, the sand will have to make its way around the big rocks. More importantly, if you cannot fit all the sand, who cares; *its only sand.*

Working on oneself is also about working on being a good person and doing the right thing. When people are polled, the number one trait they want in a friend, partner and, oh yes, in a leader, is honesty.

This was one of the biggest lessons Mike's dad instilled in him at a young age. Mike always says, "There were so many things my father instilled in me as a child that stick with me to this day. Three of them focus in this area: First, *always do the right thing.* Even if it goes against the grain, if you can put your head down on your pillow at night knowing you did the right thing, you are successful. If something is worth doing, then it is worth doing it well. Second, *always be a person of your word.* Your word is your bond. No matter what happens to you in life, this is something that can never be taken away from you. If you say you are going to do something, do it! Third, *never, ever make a promise you can't keep.* This is the kiss of death, as you will lose credibility and, most of all, *trust.* Once this is lost in your personal and professional life, you lose. Period. End of story.

"Dad was right. I have seen so many people in leadership or relationships make this mistake: They make promises they can't keep. Why do they do this? Well, that is a good question, but there are many reasons. They want you to believe in them, they are avoiding conflict, or they are just telling you what they think you want to hear. This is the biggest mistake anyone can make. So as Dad would say, be a person of your word. Labor at being a good person; in other words, truly invest in yourself and find success and balance."

This way of approaching life came out in all our interviews with every one of the people we met with. It didn't matter the person's role or background; *honesty* was top of the list for all of them in regards to their professional and personal life. Here are just two examples:

～

Gloria Greco shared a very similar story with us in regard to her father and the true meaning of success. "My father did not complete his college education and worked most of his life for his brother-in-law in the family business.

From a financial standpoint, many might not think he was 'successful,' but he had a different kind of success. He and my mother had a great marriage and raised a large family and did a lot of charity work, serving his community for years. At his wake, we were overwhelmed by the number of people that came up to us and told us about how my father impacted their lives, helped their family, found them a place to live, or helped them find a job, and the list goes on. Helping others was a real motivator for him. He added real value."

~

And here is one from General David Perkins: "I attended the funeral of a general. There was a sergeant and a corporal there that flew (on their own dime) to the funeral fifty years later to pay their respects. So here is the question: When you die, how many corporals would come to your funeral?"

~

When you talk about the 5Ls and life balance, you must talk about work-life balance. This is so critical for all of us, and most of us don't have it. A lot of the time it becomes low on the priority list. This is a critical error and fatal flaw that leads to incredible levels of stress, burnout, and an overall feeling of dissatisfaction. True work-life balance takes all 5Ls. It starts with LOVE and self-love; then LAUGHTER, with not taking yourself, your life, and your job too seriously, stress management; LABOR, working on something for you every day; LEISURE, taking time out to recharge; and LEAVE, learning how to pivot, move on, embrace change, and leave negativity behind.

If we said to you that labor can actually be a very effective tool to help you get through a difficult time in your life, would you think we were crazy? Well, for a very long time, if you had said that to Mike, he would have thought you were out of your mind. *Labor* being a positive and helping someone? Never! However, it truly can.

When he was at one of the darkest points in his life, as mentioned when his father was battling cancer and he was going through a divorce, his job became his refuge. You will see in both the LAUGHTER and LEAVE chapters that we say you can only control the controllable. There is no truer statement. He will tell you, "My job, even though I was not inspired or lifted by it, it was something I knew. I could control the outcomes, and it was familiar. It gave me the ability to turn off all the pain and craziness going on in my life and just focus on the task at hand. I worked hard to *compartmentalize* in my mind what I was letting myself think about. Believe it or not, one of the things that got me through those dark years was my job. So while I wasn't following my passion at the time, it helped me keep my sanity."

Now let's take a hard look on the negative impact of only having this one "L," LABOR, in your life, and why people will work so hard and put their job above all else. Let us know if any of these sound familiar: "If I put work above all else, it will make me indispensable"; "I will beat out the competition"; "I have too many responsibilities not to"; or "It is what will make me reach my monetary goal." Moreover, some people let their work define who they are. Your identity can never be your title or position at a company.

So let us be direct and give you some truth that you might not want to hear: *There is no such thing as being indispensable.*

When it comes to business, we are all replaceable. If you dropped dead from a heart attack because you worked yourself to death, the company will go on. One of the things that we have seen in our over seven decades combined years in business is that anyone can be replaced at any time—even the head of a company. No one—and we mean no one—is irreplaceable. So if you are defining yourself by your job, what do you think will happen to you when you lose your job and it is no longer the center of your life? What happens to your identity? What happens to your mental fitness? Think about it for a moment. Now ask yourself what your priority should be.

Let us leave you with one last very important note on LABOR, a pitfall you must watch out for that may topple your world. This is why we constantly talk about the balance being critical. If you only focused on one of the **Ls**—in this case, LABOR—in your life, *you will fail!* We cannot stress that enough. When you are obsessed with following your passion and it becomes the only thing you have in life, you run the risk of losing everything else that you worked for. Doing this will have a detrimental impact on every aspect of your life: your health, your relationships, everything. *You must have balance or you will fail.*

Here's a very personal story from Sal that is another example where the balance of the **5Ls** is missing and the lasting impact it can have if you don't right the ship and find the proper balance. In this case, we are talking about letting your job define you and the importance of learning to forgive yourself, as we mentioned in the LOVE chapter. As an example, you focus entirely on only one of the **Ls**.

"It was the fall of 1989, and I was attending the KPMG national partner's meeting in Orlando, Florida. At the time,

I was living in New York, and my parents had moved to Port Richey, Florida, about a two-hour drive from where I was in Orlando at the time. I had not seen my parents in several years. I have to say, that was my own doing, being so busy and wrapped up in my work. It was a lot easier for me to travel to see them than having them come up to New York, but I never made the time or effort. My priority was my work, and I let it define me.

"I had received a message while at my partner's meeting that my mother was ill and in the hospital in Port Richey, with no explanation or details as to why. I decided that after the meeting I would go and visit my parents—after the meeting, not immediately. Seriously? So when the meetings were over a few days later, I drove over to Port Richey. My mother was still in the hospital, and I had no clue what I would find when I got there. My father greeted me in the hallway as I walked to her room. 'Sally,' he said (the Italian way of saying Sal), 'it's not good.' 'What do you mean it's not good?' I said. 'What's going on, Dad?' Turned out my mother was diagnosed with stage four lung cancer that had metastasized and reached her brain. She was given six months to live. She was awake and vocal but did not recognize me. Her brain wasn't functioning. She was so lost and confused; it broke my heart.

"My mother and I used to have intellectual discussions and debates on just about any topic, but no more. Suddenly those days were gone forever. She didn't even remember my name. All her thoughts were so jumbled, so confused. I could see her trying hard to get the words together, but her brain wasn't making the connection. I lost her. I remember her asking me if I won today. *Won, Mom? Won what?* Her brain was stuck in my high school days when I was playing soccer at Bishop Riley High School. So I played along and told her, 'Yeah. We played and we won.' I had really lost her. I started to cry but didn't want her to see me that way. I gotta tell you, for one of the first times in my life I wasn't in control.

"At that point, I was so angry at myself for not taking the time to be more in touch with her. I remember asking my father when this started happening and why wasn't I told. He said, 'I didn't want to bother you because I know how busy you are at work.' Was it that obvious? I was guilty of letting my work define me and control my own life. I was so focused on LABOR. My own 5Ls were out of whack. I lost the 5Ls balance. I only had one, and it was on steroids!

"I chose not to be there during her hospice days. I was swamped at work and under a client deadline that couldn't be missed.

"Mom passed away just a little over a month from that visit with her. I was back in New York when I got the call regarding her passing. It was Sunday, December 3 at one o'clock, on a very cold December day. I was just about to sit down and watch my Giants play the Eagles. I remember that after getting the call from my sister—who stayed with my mom during her hospice days—that Mom had passed away, I went for a walk, a *very long* walk. I had walked from my house in Bayside, NY, where I was living with my then wife and son, to my childhood house in Flushing several miles away. It felt like I was going home. I was sort of numb and didn't feel the freezing cold a bit. Maybe I was trying to bring back or relive some of our special days together, the good old days that were gone.

"I am so embarrassed to be actually writing this, but the next day was Monday, and I went to my office at 345 Park Avenue. Sometimes we use our job, our workplace, as a security blanket. For me, it was what I knew best and where I was the most comfortable. I had a client deadline to meet, and I wasn't going to miss it. It is as clear as day to me now, as if it was yesterday. I got to the office and told Jake, one of my partners and good friend, that my mother had passed away yesterday. He was shocked that I was in the office. 'What the hell are you doing here?' Jake asked. I told him I had to get a client's audit report out the door by the end of the week. The next thing I knew, there was a knock on my office door; it was the managing partner of the firm. He entered my office, closed the door and said, 'I heard about your mother's death. I'm so sorry for your loss. What in God's name are you doing here?' I remember saying, 'Herb, I've got to get a report out by the end of this week.' 'No, you don't,' Herb said. 'Go home, Sal. It's not that important. Right now your family is your priority, and that's what is important. You need to be there for them.'

"I left the office, went home and made the necessary arrangements to get to Florida and be with my family. As I write this, I have such a feeling of regret that I missed the signs. I missed the clear signals of not having my 5Ls in the proper balance. The importance of reminding yourself daily to have each of the 5Ls in your life can't be overstated.

"It's over thirty years later, and I still remember it like it was yesterday. We all live with regrets, but as we said earlier, learning to truly forgive helps to lessen them. Remember our self-love discussion? It's an integral part of self-love. Please take it from me: *You can live with failure in your life, but you can't live with regret.*

"Remember what I mentioned earlier in this chapter about my granddaughter Giuliana telling me, 'Grandpa, do like me do'? Again, I say to you, 'Please don't do like me do.' Don't let your job or LABOR define you. Always labor on not letting one "L" dominate your life. *Live the 5Ls balance.*"

As we did in the LOVE and LAUGHTER sections, take a quick second to think of the color that comes to mind when you hear the word *Labor*. Remember that for the end of the book.

~

As I mentioned in the previous chapters, here is our **5Ls** Self-Assessment Tool. Answer yes or no to these ten simple questions as honestly as you can. If the question is something you are on the fence about or have just somewhat in your life, then the answer should be "No." If you have less than seven "Yes" answers, that is an indicator that you need to work on this particular "**L**" to find your **5Ls** balance.

LABOR

"Y"	"N"	
		Do I have passion and purpose in what I do?
		Do I work on something that's just for me every day?
		Do I see value in what I do?
		Do I realize that a successful relationship requires work?
		Do I work at taking time out for the important people in my life?
		Do I set personal & professional goals and work at attaining them?
		Do I implement action plans to make positive change in my life?
		Do I work on prioritizing what is important in my life?
		Do I invest in myself daily?
		Do I feel joy in my achievements?

CHAPTER FOUR

LEISURE

"Almost everything will work if you unplug it for
a few minutes...including you."

—Anne Lamott

Leisure has often been defined as free time—freedom from work, school, or other responsibilities and tasks. We define LEISURE as *the need to find time to disconnect and recharge ourselves. You need to find your Me Time as Clearer Minds = Better Decisions.* This Me Time allows you take a step out of the physical and mental stress of the day. This is time you carve out for yourself when you shut off the pressures of life, something you do just for you. It could also include some time off in your day with the person you love. This could be called your "We Time." Before you read further, we want you to really reflect on the answers to the following questions: How do you look at *leisure*? Is it positive or negative? Do you see investing in leisure as a strength or weakness or perhaps as a waste, or does it have guilt implications? When you think of the word *leisure*, what are some of the first thoughts that come to mind?

When you visualize leisure, do you think of being lazy? Lounging around doing nothing? Sleeping in or not being productive? *Lazy* has a negative connotation, doesn't it?

Most of the time when the question "Do you see LEISURE as a positive or negative?" is posed in one of our trainings or seminars, usually everyone responds with the immediate knee-jerk reaction, "It's a positive!" Would you agree with them? Well then, the next question we ask is "How many of you use all your time off every year?" Most of the time, if we are lucky, maybe one or two people raise their hand. So if taking time out for yourself is such a positive, then why are you not taking it?

Mike would tell you he worked for a company that had a use-it-or-lose-it policy for time off. Every year he left most of it on the table.

So why is that, if we think that leisure is so positive? Well, most people make excuses and sacrifice their time off, or even just a few moments of time out, to the other seemingly more important things in their life. We hear this all the time: "I can't take off; my role is too important"; "I can't take off; things would fall apart"; "I can't take off; things are way too busy." The excuses go on and on. Sound a little familiar?

LEISURE plays right into LOVE, self-love to be exact. We talked about this in the prior chapters. But as with all the Ls, it overlaps into all 5Ls. You will see why as you read on. But first we want you to change your perspective and take a new approach to leisure. We want you to look at leisure as self-investment. We know what you are thinking: *self-investment*? Yes, self-investment. As we discussed with the Oxygen Mask Theory, self-investment is the most important action you can take on the road to a balanced and successful life.

Taking time to disconnect and recharge is critical to every aspect of your life. Doing this helps you manage stress, avoid burnout, and function at your highest level. There are so many things in your life that you cannot control, but you can and must control your Me Time. If you are like most people, you never let your electronics lose battery life. You take time every day to recharge your phone, your laptop, and your other devices, right? What happens to these items when the battery gets low? They don't perform to their top capacity. What happens if you let the battery totally run out? They die, right? They stop working. It is the same for you! *Are you telling us that your devices are more important than you?* You also need to recharge your battery to be able to perform at your best so as not to crash and burn. You need to find your Me Time every day just to handle the pressures of life. It could be time off or a vacation, but it could also be as simple as taking a walk, reading a book, meditation, or riding a bike. You get the idea. It can also be taking a few moments to do some deep breathing to reset. Me Time is different for everyone because *you* define it. You need to find what your Me Time is and enjoy it every day. Use that amazing calendar app on your phone and create an appointment for you. Make that Me Time appointment your top priority. Protect it like it's the most important meeting of the day, because *guess what, it is!*

~

As so well stated by Regina Bei during our interview, "I now know I need to stay focused on my Me Time. I now make time for yoga, exercise, and time with friends. It has totally changed my life."

~

Rande Bynum gave us insight into her definition during our interview. She shared, "My Me Time is reading. I love reading. I have over two thousand books at my house. My father loved books. Every wall in my house had books. At one point, my mother said to my father that he could no longer bring books into our home. When my father passed, we found books stashed, hidden all over the house and in his car. He was sneaking books into the house! That is where I get it from. I even have a reading chair. Reading not only allows you to escape but to time travel. It is my favorite, favorite thing to do. It is a horrible dating profile answer. Reading allows me to forget where I am. I love to travel and have been all over the world. Reading allows you to travel to the past or the future. I just love people's stories. It relaxes me and reenergizes me. I can actually remember the day I got my library card."

~

Okay, now that we've covered that, let's be honest; how often do you take time for you? How often do you shut off and enjoy who you are and where you are in your life? When you do take off, do you feel guilty? Are you always checking emails? Are you worrying about what is going on at the office? What about at night or over the weekends, are you still connected to your job? Why is this?

Well, there is the misconception that always being in the office or on call is a sign of strength, commitment, or you feel you must do this to stay ahead of the competition. So we will be brutally honest with you: If you really think about it, *you do it because you care too much about what people think.* Ponder that for a moment.

The real miss here is that you are actually *more productive* if you take time to recharge your batteries. It has been proven over and over again, yet people don't take that time for themselves. The Japanese actually have a word for it called "Karoshi." Loosely translated, it means "overwork death." People are actually dying from working too hard—plugging away and not investing in themselves. Never finding their Me Time or making it a priority.

A recent study from the World Health Organization found that working long hours, such as fifty-five hours a week, causes a 35 percent higher risk for stroke and 17 percent higher risk of dying from ischemic heart disease, compared to working thirty to forty hours a week.

On the flip side, a study quoted by *Harvard Health Publishing* showed that people who took fewer than ten of their vacation days per year had a 34.6 percent likelihood of receiving a raise or bonus in a three-year period of time. People who took more than ten of their vacation days had a 65.4 percent chance of receiving a raise or bonus. Why do you think that is? It is because they took the time to recharge and then brought their *best self to work*.

Even though some people know the benefits of recharging, they are still not taking that much-needed time out. A recent article regarding a survey done on work-life balance from priceline.com spoke right to the issue of the lack of time off. Here are just a few stats they quoted:

- Only one in five Americans (20 percent) used all their paid time off (PTO) in 2020, down from 30 percent in 2019, with 30 percent holding off—hoping they'd be able to travel later—and 28 percent planning to carry over their unused days.

- Many also felt that they couldn't take time off because their company was too busy for them to be away (19 percent), or they wanted to save their PTO in case they or a loved one got sick (29 percent).

- In a prior survey, Priceline found that just one in five (20 percent) had regrets about how they used PTO in 2019. However, in 2021, half (54 percent) of the Americans who didn't use all their days off regret not taking more time off in 2020.

This is a real problem and a total lack of self-love. We have been in executive leadership roles for over seventy years combined, traveling all over the world. We have managed and hired thousands of employees in our tenure. One of the things we have seen people negotiate when getting a new job is for more time off. Yet they don't use it. This is just mind-boggling. It is obviously very important, yet the statistics show people are just not taking the time to disconnect and recharge.

We are just as guilty of this practice. We both were huge offenders of not taking time off and used all the same excuses listed above. We thought it was our edge; it was what kept us ahead of the pack. We had to; it's what the role called for, and we were too important to be out. *What a load of crap!*

∼

During our interview with Richard Catalano, he made it very clear that "Americans are weekend worriers. We work all week and pack our weekends. We need to recharge our batteries on a more consistent basis. This is the key to avoiding burnout."

∼

As Mike mentioned before, he blamed part of the reason he never took time off and never being around on feeling bound by the Golden Handcuffs. He would tell you, "I was going to get the C-level title if it killed me. The scary part is, I got my 'C' title, and it almost did [kill me] by negatively impacting my health and every part of my life. Smart move, Mannix. It was only after that inflection point in my life that I told you is when I finally started to get my priorities straight. I needed to take the time to be with my children more. Prior to that, I was working so hard, trying to give them the things I didn't have, that I was never around for them. Even when I was there for them, I was not. I was constantly checking email and messages—day, night, and weekends, getting on conference calls over vacations and never being truly present. Talk about regret that still haunts me when I think about it."

Here is another true story from my past that you probably think I am making up, but the sad part is, I'm not. Please don't think less of me, but here it goes. "I was traveling this one year more than usual. I came home one day from yet again another long business trip. As I walked through the door, my daughter, Sarah, who was almost five at the time, didn't recognize me and ran away yelling, 'stranger danger!'—something the kids were taught at school to avoid people they didn't know taking them. My own daughter didn't recognize me. This made me sick to my stomach. Now, to be fair, I came home a day early and had a hat and overcoat on, but that's not the point. It really happened.

"Now my beautiful daughter is twenty-one and about to graduate from an Ivy League school that I could only have dreamed of getting into and is one of the most incredible people I know. Since becoming a single parent and finally getting my act together, I have been involved in every aspect of her life, and I'm blessed to have an amazing relationship with her. But I have to tell you, before that life-changing event, this jerk missed her kindergarten graduation to do a contract renewal for a big client. Something I will never get back and still bothers me to this day.

"It wasn't just my children; I was absent for everyone, even if I was physically there or not. This example is going to get me in trouble with my 'now' wife, but it's important for you to hear. While on my honeymoon, second marriage mind you, on the beautiful Hawaiian island of Kauai, I would sneak off to hide in closets or the bathroom to answer emails because I thought that's what I needed to do as the Chief Sales Officer. I finally got my 'C' title, and I could never disconnect—or at least that is what I told myself. What drugs was I on? What a freaking idiot! Didn't I learn anything?!

"Now here is the crazy part of the story. When I finally did get my act together and started taking time for myself and the ones I loved, my career actually improved. I was more productive, engaged, and more successful than ever before. Sounds crazy, right? Well, it's 100 percent true and is right in line with the statistics. Please learn from my mistakes. Take time out for you and the ones you love. Again, please hear me when I say to you, you are worth it."

What we have seen and experienced is the sacrificing of Me Time for work time—usually in the early stages of a career to prove that you are dedicated—gets rewarded. This contributes to the wrong mindset of thinking that leisure, or taking time off, equals a waste of time, lack of productivity, and commitment.

Here is something else to think about and is part of the problem of why disconnecting is such an issue here in the US. We Americans call time off "vacation," the definition of it being "a period spent away from home or business in travel or recreation." Okay, not bad, but could be better. So again, let's take a different approach. Outside the United States some people call it "holiday." Think about that word for a moment: holiday. Now let's look at that definition: "a time of festivity or celebration when no work is done." Yes! Why don't we celebrate ourselves more? We need to go on holiday. We need to realize that PTO is not "Pretend Time Off."

It is also critical to your mental and spiritual health that when you are taking this time off, you break it into two sections, time for you and time with the ones you love. But you need to be investing in yourself. What we mean by this is, when you are not at work, you need to be *not at work*. Do something you love that refuels your mind, body, and soul. This dedication to yourself will make you more effective in every aspect of your life. You will be in a better emotional state. Your well-being, mental wellness, and fitness will improve, and you will be a better person in general. Sound crazy? Give it a try, and you will be amazed at how quickly you will see the difference.

The next part of the equation is, now that you are in a better state of mind, LEISURE with the ones you love. It will bond you and build memories that will last a lifetime. It is not about the amount of years that you live but *really living the years you have.*

As discussed earlier, this commitment to yourself needs to be a daily activity. Most people think their Me Time needs to be later in the day. This is another mistake, as covered in

LAUGHTER, Setting the Tone in every aspect of your life. You should start this right out of the gate.

One of the many tools we teach in our trainings is *setting a morning routine*. How many of you out there use your phone as your alarm clock? A lot of people do. This is a bad move. What happens is, the phone is next to your bed. It leads you to look at it all hours of the night and morning. Does this habit sound familiar: Your alarm goes off, you grab your phone to stop it, then you look at your emails or your social media? You are not even vertical, and you are letting the world and the stress in. *Stop it!* Mike will tell you, "I was told about setting a morning routine a few years ago. It has totally helped me handle stress and set a positive tone for the day. I do not use my phone as an alarm. When my alarm goes off, the first thing I do is drink a huge bottle of water. This gets me hydrated and gets the sleep out and my brain functioning. It also helps if I have been having too much fun the night before. I then work out for at least twenty minutes, then journal or meditate, or I do all three. If I only have time for one of the three, I exercise no matter what. I give myself the first forty-five to sixty minutes of the day. This is my Me Time. After this, I am in a much better head space to take on the day."

Okay, so let's stay on that subject for a bit. We know that we are going to lose some of you here, but exercise is key critical—period—and is a needed example of Me Time. Most people look at exercise as work; and you probably think this needs to be under LABOR, right? Wrong! You need to look at exercise as very important Me Time.

Having LEISURE in your life and taking care of yourself physically and mentally is the foremost important component to leading a happy, successful, and balanced life. You can pick up any magazine while sitting in a doctor's office, turn on the TV, or look online, and it screams about the benefits of nutrition and exercise to personal health and well-being. Countless studies over the decades have proven time and time again that exercise and a proper diet not only improves your physical health but extends your life and improves mental health. Exercise will give you a clearer mind. It's not a cliché that Clearer Minds = Better Decisions; it's the truth. Have you ever made a big decision when you are emotional or burned out? Was it a good one? Probably not. Just look at the quote from Anne Lamott, "Almost everything will work if you unplug it for a few minutes...including you."

For many years, Mike was a Certified Personal Trainer along with being a martial arts instructor. He could literally write a separate book just on the importance of this subject and its benefits. But let's not just take his word for it. If you were to google the benefits of exercise, there would be millions of articles and studies that pop up. Here are just two:

- Recent research has shown that regular exercise affects much more than physical strength, weight loss, and cardiovascular health. A number of studies have shown clear benefits in memory and brain function, post-treatment fatigue, recurrent malignancy, and the risk of new cancers. fredhutch.org.

- A long-term study out of the Mayo Clinic took a deep dive into just some of the many benefits. At a high level, they discussed how exercise controls weight, combats countless health conditions and diseases, improves mood and self-esteem, boosts energy, promotes better sleep, can put the spark back into your sex life, and can not only be fun but improve relationships.

You need to commit to yourself that you will exercise at least twenty minutes a day. That's not a lot in a twenty-four-hour day to find twenty minutes for your Me Time and your ultimate success. Remember, you are worth it! You will hear us say that phrase a lot. We hope it is sinking in.

So why with all this proven data do people not take time to execute this critical step? Bottom line is—and we hate to be blunt—excuses and lack of self-love. People make up excuses so that when they fail, get sick, or gain weight, they can point the blame somewhere else, such as:

- There is just not enough time in the day.
- Healthy food is just too expensive.
- I'm way too busy; who has time to exercise?
- I'm too old to work out.
- I don't know how.
- I'm too lazy.
- I'm too tired.
- I have too many other important things that need to come first.

And the list of excuses goes on and on. Do any of these sound familiar?

If you don't believe us, ask any medical professional, and they will tell you the same. So stop making excuses, take ownership, and make time to exercise and eat right. It will not only help you look and feel better, you will have a much better quality of life on multiple levels.

Me Time is even more critical during a stressful or crisis period in your life. This is when you need to recharge your batteries the most. Just like we told you in LOVE, you need to be asking yourself every day, *What am I doing for me today*? Here is a little tip: Write that question on something and put it where you will see it every day. Doesn't matter where or on what, as long as it smacks you in the face on a regular basis. Doing this will help you stay focused on it.

LEISURE is also critical in the workplace. It cannot be all work all the time. Having fun and taking time out from the day to day at work builds trust, comradery, an environment of acceptance, and increases the productivity of your team tenfold.

Let's switch gears for a moment and discuss how LEISURE can help you and your team in the workplace on multiple levels. Let's look at *leisure* being the same as *play*. With the increase of work-from-home and employees now demanding better work-life balance due to the COVID-19 pandemic, employers are incorporating more virtual playtime in their weekly programs. Effective employee engagement is no longer just nice to have; it is a must-have to keep teams engaged, retained, and feeling that their company is invested in their well-being and mental fitness. It has become the difference between success and failure for leaders, management, and organizations to reach their goals.

A recent article published by the Association for Psychological Science (APS) has found evidence that play at work, or "work-play," is linked with less fatigue, boredom, stress, and burnout in individual workers. Work-play is positively associated with job satisfaction, retention, and productivity.

Teams of workers can benefit from work-play via increased trust, bonding, social interaction, and a decreased sense of hierarchy. Furthermore, findings suggest that having fun at work can benefit whole organizations by creating a friendlier work atmosphere, higher employee commitment to work, more flexible organization-wide decision-making, and increased organizational creativity.

Work-play has also been proven to improve retention in learning. That is why when you are training your team, you need to make it fun. There are three main ways people learn:

- **Kinesthetic (physical) Learning** — performing the task.

- **Visual Learning** — reading or watching something being performed.

- **Auditory Learning** — listening to the information.

Work-play encompasses all three. It is also critical to keeping your audience's attention. Have you ever been in a lecture, on a webinar, or participating in a presentation that is essentially nothing more than *death by PowerPoint*? If you are honest, you might have picked up maybe 10 percent (if you were still awake or had your camera on) of what they were trying to get across. Now on the flip side, have you ever learned something new and had fun while doing it? We will place money on the fact that you remember most of it—if not, at least 90 percent. Injecting fun into teaching situations dramatically increases engagement, memory, and retention. The reason for this is when you are having fun, it creates a stronger pathway in your brain to long-term memory. This is not opinion; *it's science.*

In keeping with the work theme, now let us discuss leisure and boundaries. First, let's start with you. We hope that after everything we've discussed, when you are off work, you disconnect. You must set these boundaries and hold them. Once your employer or colleagues feel they can get you anytime day or night no matter what, they will. So make sure you respectfully set these boundaries. You deserve time off and, more importantly, true work-life balance. Unless it is truly life or death, you need that time to recharge and should not be disturbed. When someone calls us and says, "I'm sorry to call you, but..." we respond with, "Is it life or death?" Bottom line is, they are not sorry they called, because they just did. Now, if you are in management, you need to do the same for your team. You need to respect their boundaries the same way. The benefits for you and your team will range from stress management, mental fitness, improved performance, and employee retention.

Leisure, recharging your batteries, finding time to disconnect, having fun, and finding your Me Time is a critical component for stress reduction. When you are enjoying yourself, your body releases endorphins, changing your current state of mind from negative to a happier, positive state of mind. With all that said, having LEISURE as your Me Time, and balancing that with the other 5Ls is critical for success and for getting through stressful and difficult times that you might face in your life.

As Sal will now tell you, "You need to make Me Time a priority in your life. Fortunately or unfortunately, depending on how you look at it, I was traveling internationally for business at a fairly young age. Having only dreamed about traveling throughout Europe and seeing cities such as London, Paris, Rome, and Berlin, actually physically being there should have been a thrill of a lifetime for me. Especially for a kid (or "Sally boy") from the Bronx, NY. So there I would be in one of these great international cities on business, and I would not take any time to visit or sightsee or just take it all in. I was always afraid that if I asked for the time, it might appear that I had other things on my mind other than the business reason for being there. All business all the time. Really?

"I remember being driven around by the company driver, and he would say, 'Mr. LaGreca, over there is the Eiffel Tower,' or 'Big Ben,' or 'the Colosseum'—or whatever famous landmark or tourist spot it was—'Would you care to stop and get out to take a photo or visit?' 'No, thank you' would be my standard response. I would be sitting in the car thinking 'Wow, that's the Roman Colosseum,' and I would picture in my mind how cool it would be just to touch it or get close to it. But no. My idea was a drive-by business-like-attitude approach, as if I was too important to waste my precious time on sightseeing when deep down inside I wanted to be there. Looking back, I think how foolish I was not to take a little time and take it all in and find the time to relax and enjoy and clear my mind. So silly. Now I don't think twice about driving to the beach to feel the breeze, smell the fresh air, and grab some Me Time."

~

You have now seen throughout the book how all 5Ls overlap, intertwine, and support each other. Candice Corby told us how LEISURE and Me Time actually have taught her valuable lessons that she applies to her work life (LABOR) and how to adjust her sails, or pivot (LEAVE). "I like to cook. But I also love to garden. I'll share a metaphor with you about my leisure and how it also helps me in business. I'm not sure how much you know about rose bushes. I love rose bushes. What I have learned is February and March is when you need to prune rose bushes. Pruning is key to keeping them healthy as they grow and mature. Sometimes they have a branch that used to be the best branch on that rose bush and produced beautiful blooms. But at some point, it might encounter an obstacle in its life. There might be a drought, or it might have had a disease due to overwatering or under-watering that affects the branch. So what used to be the best branch is now hurting it. The bush will do everything it can to make that branch well again. It will send all the sustenance of the plant to try and save that branch instead of developing new growth, impacting the development of the other branches. Sometimes you have to prune for things to continue to grow and succeed.

"I have pivoted a couple of times in the past prior to Cobra Legal Solutions. I left big law in New York and started a cheese shop. Then I pivoted again from there to start and be the CEO at Cobra. Like the rose bush, sometimes to continue to grow you must leave something that was working great before but may not be working now."

~

As we bring the chapter to a close, let's look at another perspective to LEISURE and time to recharge. As we pointed out, it doesn't need to be a big vacation far away or cost a lot. It can also be with someone else. We like to call this We

Time. Bottom line, Me Time is anytime you just shut off the world and recharge your batteries and refuel your soul.

One of the ways the Mannix boys would practice Me Time was a trip once a year to Maine. "When I was growing up, my father, as I mentioned earlier, worked two jobs and was a volunteer Captain for the Coram Fire Department. Needless to say, growing up I didn't get to spend a lot of time with him. Now, I'm not pretending it was like the song by Harry Chapin, 'Cats in the Cradle,' but time with Dad was not as much as I would have liked until I graduated college. Dad had this passion for Maine and for sailing. His dream was to buy a vacation home in Maine, buy a sailboat or, God willing, to have both. I also have always found true peace when I was out on the water in any way, shape, or form. Didn't matter to me; I have always been able to disconnect and recenter when I was on or by the water.

"One day, a few years after graduating college and moving out of my parents' house, my Dad called me up and said, 'Want to run something past you. I am going for my sailing license; would you want to do it with me? Also, I want to start traveling up to Maine to drive the coast once a year just to get away. What do you think, just you and me?' In my mind, this was nothing short of the best idea ever, and I responded with, 'I would really love that, Dad.'

"A month later we took our first sailing lesson together. It was a cold, rainy September day. We got up at 5:00 a.m. and met at the sailing school in Greenport, Long Island. The wind was blowing hard, and the bay actually had whitecaps. Most people would have probably turned around, but there was no way I was; this was time with Dad. The class broke up into five teams and boarded five keel boats. In only a few minutes after casting off, we raised the sails and the boat heeled hard. That was it; Dad and I were hooked. The feeling of freedom, even with the painful pelting rain and ice-cold wind, was nothing we had ever experienced, and our minds cleared of any stress or worries we had. This was our Me Time and our We Time, and we would get out on the water as much as we could after this day.

"But this was nothing compared to our trips to Maine. It is almost impossible to put into words how much those trips did for the both of us. Every year for eighteen years, shortly after we started our sailing adventures, Dad and I would pack up his car and drive from his house on the east end of Long Island, along the coast, all the way up to the top of Maine. Most people that take a getaway have a destination and everything planned out. Not us. The *joy* of the trip was just the two of us traveling leisurely up the coast, stopping along the way to discover new towns. My dad loved the adventure of just turning off at a random exit and making our way along some road to a place we had never been before. However, we had one town that was our favorite—Camden, Maine—and it eventually would become our home base during these trips in the later years, especially when Dad got sick.

"I remember the feeling of joy when we would pass the sign entering our happy place, Welcome to Camden—Maine the way life should be. It was like the weight of the world would lift off our shoulders. We would get almost giddy with excitement. This is a picture-perfect New England town that was established in 1791. It has winding roads with quaint shops and restaurants that overlook Camden's port. This picturesque place also has a charming stream that snakes through the heart of town and empties into Camden Harbor with a waterfall. Our favorite spot was on this hill that overlooks the entire town and the marina. It sits up high with beautiful wooden benches and gorgeous flowered bushes of every color. The waterfront is filled with some of the most amazing large wooden sailing ships from all over the world.

"My dad and I would love to go out on a day sail and help crew one of these perfectly restored 150-year-old ships. We would look forward to these trips every year like it was Christmas. They truly were a gift, a gift of a break from everything and everyone, time to recharge and refuel our souls. Sometimes I would literally count down the months and days till our next trip. I am not exaggerating when I say *this was our medicine.* Just the few short days we had together would change our entire perspective. It cured us of all that was weighing on our minds, as it cleared them totally. It made us better people, as once recharged, we could bring our best selves back to our families, friends, and work. It was the purest definition of Me Time."

We have laid out a lot of scientific data on the health benefits of Me Time and looking at it as an investment in you. All that data is great, but let me leave you with this personal experience on the healing power of LEISURE, if I might.

"On the last trip to Maine, Dad was too sick to drive. He had lost so much weight, and his strength was waning. He looked so fragile and frail and was almost unrecognizable from the man I knew. For this last trip, I flew us into Portland, Maine, and rented a car. I looked at my father and said, 'Dad, I got this. It's my turn to drive you. Just sit back, rest, and enjoy.' He smiled, and we got on our way. As we neared the entrance of the town and saw that Camden sign, my father went from being hunched over to sitting up straight with his eyes wide open. We parked at the hotel, and he leaped from the car. He looked at me with this magical excitement and said, 'Let's not waste a moment checking in; let's walk to the town right now.' Now keep in mind he could barely walk, I had to help him in and out of the car, and he really didn't have an appetite anymore, being so sick from the chemo and the cancer. I said, 'Okay, Dad, let's do it.'

"He was like a kid in a candy shop, darting from store to store, touching mostly everything, as if to see if they were real. After two hours into this he said, 'When are we shoving off on our schooner?' I fumbled to answer, as I had not booked one because of his health. I didn't want to disappoint him so I said, 'Soon, Dad, soon. Do you want to try to grab some lunch first?' I then got an answer I did not expect, 'Absolutely! I am starving. I want a giant bowl of clam chowder!' You could have knocked me over with a feather, as even the smell of food would make him nauseous at times.

"I took him to our favorite place in town and set him up on the back deck overlooking the entire harbor. I excused myself and pretended to take a call. I did a mad scramble out of the restaurant down to the dock to find one of the Captains. Running up and down the docks, I found one last schooner that was going out for the day. I grabbed the Captain, explained the situation with my father's health, and asked if he could please fit us on. He looked at me, put his hand on my shoulder and said, 'It would be an honor to have him on board. We leave in an hour.' I could not thank him enough, and ran back to the restaurant. I walked up and sat down. Dad had already finished his soup and was looking for something else to eat. He turned to me and said, 'I want to go to our favorite place for dinner tonight, the Whale's Tooth Inn. I really want their lobster and prime rib.' In total disbelief, I hugged him and said, 'That would be fantastic; I would love that.' I had to turn away for a moment, as I needed to compose myself.

"After Dad finished his sandwich, which I had no idea he had even ordered, we headed to the boat. The Captain greeted my father as if he had known him forever. He shook my father's hand and said, 'It's an honor to have you sailing with us today, Mr. Mannix! Welcome aboard.' The crew started to scurry around the deck and cast off the lines. We slowly pulled away from the dock and headed out of the harbor under power. The first mate tapped me on the shoulder and asked if I would like to help him hoist the mainsail. If you know me, that is not even a question. I responded, 'Absolutely!' and we both worked the sail together; the other sails went up after. The Captain killed the engine, everything went silent, and the boat started to heel as the wind took over. It was magical. I turned back to look at my dad, and what I didn't know was that the Captain had asked him if he wanted to take the helm for a bit. Just as I turned, I saw my dad's hands grasp the wheel.

"Now, whether or not *you believe in miracles*, I can tell you I witnessed one that day. My father stood erect with a strength I hadn't seen in almost two years. His face literally transformed back to the man I knew all my life. It was him, not the man battling cancer. My hero was at the helm doing what he loved.

"After his turn at the wheel he came and sat next to me. 'I can't tell you how good I feel right now,' he said with a smile that just beamed. I responded, 'Me too, Dad, me too.' One of the other passengers asked me if we wanted them to take a picture of us with my camera. Dad responded with a big, 'Yes. That would be great!' before I could even look up. The wife of the couple took our picture of our perfect moment in time, which now sits in a place I can see in my house every day. She handed me back the camera and I thanked her. We then turned and stared at the horizon.

"Just like anything you love, the trip was over in the blink of an eye. As we were leaving, the Captain once again came up to my father and said, 'Thank you for sailing with us today. You two can crew my boat any time you want.' My father turned to him and said, 'Save a spot for us this time next year. We will be back!' Once again, I turned my head to compose myself.

"Later that night we had our last dinner at the Whale's Tooth. It was a perfect Maine night. The sky was huge, the moon lit up the water, and you could see every star. They gave us our usual seat overlooking the ocean. The server who came up knew us well from our many trips over the years. She turned to my dad and exclaimed, 'Oh my God! Mr. Mannix! So good to have you back! Do you know what you want or do you need time?' With the biggest smile I had ever seen, he responded with, 'We will both have the surf and turf. Oh yes, and we will have the baked clams as an appetizer.' I almost fell out of my seat. Dad could barely finish one meal a day, but he was going all in. He looked at me and said, 'I'm starving.'

"I had never been so happy. It was almost like he was cured. The food came, and we looked out over the water as we ate our meals fit for a king. The sea sparkled as the lobster boats bobbed up and down. The wind was cool and blew softly. I don't think the moon could have gotten any bigger. Time began to slow down. It was like nothing I have experienced since. As we finished, my dad looked at me, put his hand on my arm and said, 'I will miss this. I love you, son. Thank you.' Just for a brief moment, I had my father back on that trip."

And that is the true power of the **5Ls**.

As we had you do in the LOVE, LAUGHTER, and LABOR sections, take a quick second to think of the color that comes to mind when you hear the word *Leisure*. Remember that for later.

~

Answer yes or no to these ten simple questions as honestly as you can. If the question is something you are on the fence about or have just somewhat in your life, then the answer should be "No." If you have less than seven "Yes" answers, that is an indicator that you need to work on this particular "L" to find your 5Ls balance.

LEISURE

"Y"	"N"	
		Do I know what my "ME TIME" really is?
		Do I use my "ME TIME" to disconnect and recharge on a daily basis?
		Do I look at LEISURE as an investment in me?
		Do I exercise more than 20 minutes daily?
		Do I put my phone down and find time to be in the moment?
		Do I meditate, journal or use stress management tools daily?
		Do I take actions that nurture my mental well-beig?
		Do I realize that when I am not at work, I am not at work?
		Do I use all my time off?
		Do I realize that Clearer Minds = Better Decisions?

CHAPTER FIVE

LEAVE

"Don't cry because it's over. Smile because it happened."

—Dr. Suess

LEAVE is about *managing and embracing change. Knowing how to pivot and adjust the sails.* Knowing when to move on from something and leave it behind for many of us can be very difficult and quite frightening. For some people this is the toughest of all the **5Ls**. However, LEAVE is not just about leaving a relationship, a bad situation or a job; it can be about leaving a bad decision. Knowing when something is over, not working out and is time to move on can be a challenge, to say the least. The worst thing that any of us can do is stay with a bad decision because it is something you have become comfortable with. We call this Familiar Misery, and we will talk about that later in the chapter. A key concept is, once you have made the decision to change, you must learn to forgive yourself in the wake of a poor decision, as these are our greatest learning lessons. Failure, like change, is something to be embraced.

It has been said that the word F.A.I.L. means "First Attempt In Learning." To help you mentally distance yourself from the decision, try journaling about your situation, being honest about what you are experiencing and feeling. Remember, you need to learn from your decisions and use it as a momentum builder. For every poor decision you will make, you are going to make a good one. Do not let your thoughts over a decision to leave control you. Stay focused on the fact that brighter days are coming. As Dr. Suess so eloquently stated, "Don't cry because it's over; smile because it happened."

As mentioned, what you might not realize when you hear a word is not only does it elicit an emotional response, you also unknowingly equate it to a color, a color of how you feel about that thought or word. This is why we asked you at the end of every chapter (in the self-assessment section) what color came to mind when you heard that particular "L."

So now let's do that same quick exercise one last time. Take a moment. Don't think; just respond. What is the first color that comes to mind when you hear the word *Leave*? So now that you have the color, hold on to it for the moment. The color that came to mind, was it dark or light? We do this visualization exercise with our audiences, interviewees, and students during our training sessions on a regular basis. The same question is posed for each of the 5Ls. Do you remember your answers?

For LOVE, we usually get red, like *valentines*. For LAUGHTER, it's usually a *happy color*, mostly orange, as it is seen as a positive. LABOR is dark blue on a consistent basis, being related to blue collar or something that is *toiled on*. LEISURE is predominantly green, as people think of vacation, *green fields, or money being spent*. When we ask people what color immediately comes to mind for the word

LEAVE, the most popular answer we get *is a dark color,* black being what we hear most. The reason for this is the thought of leaving or change is being associated with something *dark, negative, and scary.* Some people even view *leave* or *leaving* as a death or end of something. Most recently, we did this with one of our training events. When asked the question, a student responded with the color red. Sal and I were quite surprised, as we have never heard that response. When we asked why red, she said "Because the word *leave* makes me think of someone leaving a relationship, and it makes me feel anger." The fact that this word actually elicited an emotion that was so negative and seen as abandonment was a real eye opener. This was a very different and insightful view of LEAVE.

Through our research and interviews, we have also found that individuals who are the most comfortable with change will respond with a light color, usually yellow or white. These individuals are also high achievers and able to adapt in both their personal and professional life. They view LEAVE as positive, *embrace change,* and see it as an opportunity for growth, coupled with the excitement of doing something different. We found them to be more confident and were usually focused on all **5Ls**, as they saw this as the key for success. To find true balance in your life, you must learn to embrace change. Change continuously happens and is as constant as time. You're probably familiar with the saying "There are three things you can count on in life: death, taxes, and change." So knowing this will continue to happen, if you don't learn to use change as a tool for your benefit, you will constantly experience dissatisfaction with your situation.

~

In our interview with Meg Mansell, former BET executive and now an owner of Papillon Homes, she told us that she would go out of her way to put herself in uncomfortable positions so that she could grow. She viewed change as a positive and something needed to be successful. In fact, Meg's response to the question on the color she thought of when she heard the word *leave* was pink. Can't get much brighter on the color pallet. She told us that her favorite quote is "Pressure makes diamonds." She also went on to say, "If you truly want to continue to grow and be successful, you need to stop seeing change as the enemy, and embrace it."

~

So let's start there. Be honest with yourself when you thought of the color that came to mind when you heard the word *Leave*. Was it dark? Again, be honest with yourself. Do you see LEAVE as a positive or negative? Does it excite you with the potential for growth and opportunity, or does it strike fear into your heart?

If you're like most people, *leaving* is seen from a negative perspective. What we have seen through our research is that most people do not envision a bright, vibrant color. Why did you see it that way? The reason is, it all boils down to a four-letter word—a four-letter word that, if you let it, it will control your life: FEAR! The fear of what? Is it the fear of change, the fear of the *unknown*, or is it the *fear of failure*? The fear of failure can be debilitating and crippling. It has stopped some of the strongest people and greatest leaders dead in their tracks.

Ask yourself why you are afraid to fail. Really think about it. Take a step back and look at yourself in the mirror and be honest. Don't sugarcoat it. Look deep inside and answer. So are you afraid to fail? If so, why?

Let's take a deeper dive on what we found from our studies into why people are so afraid to fail and how come it is such a powerful deterrent. Here are some of the reasons we collected from our research. Does any of this sound familiar?

- I'm afraid of what people will think and say.

- I don't want to look weak or perceived as a failure.

- I don't want to let down or disappoint my family, friends, or loved ones.

- I don't want to let myself down.

- It will hurt my career path.

- I'm just scared.

We even have people tell us that they actually get themselves physically sick thinking about change and failure. The bottom line and the main reason why we fear failure is because, once again, we place way *too much importance on what people think.*

Here is another question we pose to our training sessions: Who is your biggest critic? Most, if not all, respond that *they* are their biggest critic and beat themselves up when they fail. This is a real problem. You need to stop beating yourself up. You need to be your biggest fan. If you are waiting on someone else to make you feel good about yourself or help you find balance and happiness in your life, you will be waiting a very long time. Being your biggest fan and practicing self-love is critical for growth in your life. End of story.

~

As Winston Henderson stated so well, "I am thankful for all my mentors in my life. I am even thankful for the tormentors in my life. The problem is, sometimes we become our own tormentors."

~

Here are two things we need you to take to heart to change your life. Once again, back to self-love. If you are placing your happiness on what others think, you will be perpetually miserable. Second, failure is your best teacher. Think back to what we said in the LOVE chapter, specifically the story where Mike changed jobs and was blowing it with his new team. That lesson changed the rest of his entire career and is also helping others to this day.

The issue with caring about what others think and the fear of failure, as we mentioned in LAUGHTER, has been exacerbated by the negative impact social media is having on people's feeling of self-worth. Also mentioned in LAUGHTER, social media is not reality; it is the highlight reel of someone's life, or can even be totally made up. It is usually something that screams "Isn't my life great? Look how happy and successful I am." Therein lies the problem. It's not reality, so why do you compare what we have or do to fantasy? As we said, when have you ever seen someone post something negative about themselves or their current situation? You don't; so stop measuring your worth to this fictitious standard. *No one has it all.*

Another reason people have trouble with LEAVE is because of its direct link to change. Most people, whether they will admit to it or not, are afraid of change. Change gets you outside your comfort zone. Change causes unease and uncertainty. It is that scary unknown that will keep people in a job they hate, in a bad relationship, stuck in an addiction or just in a rut. People will go out of their way to make any excuse not to change. They will even self-sabotage any effort to change just so they can say, "You see, I tried, and it just didn't work." That is Familiar Misery. Familiar Misery is basically staying in that bad situation or bad decision because it is what you know and what you have become used to. It is not good for you, but it is something that you have convinced yourself is safe: "It's okay; not the best situation, but that's all right." *No, it's not all right!* You are basically saying to yourself, "Well, at least I know this: If I make a change, it could be worse. I would rather tolerate the known as compared to trying the unknown." It's like the saying, "The devil you know is better than the devil you don't know." But in the end, *it is still the devil.* Just because you know something or it's familiar to you doesn't make it right.

The first time Sal heard of this Familiar Misery thing, he was in a therapy session many years ago and was sincerely trying to understand why he was constantly being drawn to a certain relationship—a relationship that was never going to work out or last. Nonetheless, he would be in and out of it over several years.

"I recall saying to myself, *Come on, Sal. You know this in-and-out relationship is not the healthiest relationship, and boy is it ever mentally draining,* and wishing I could just stop and press on with my life, say goodbye to it, and close the door behind me for good. But I just did not know how to do it. I explained the feeling to my therapist, as it was like playing a vinyl record on a phonograph. You place the record on the turntable, and you move the needle over to the record. The needle finds the groove and begins to play. The needle is at home in the grooves and doesn't move; it keeps playing the song. It's not until you get up, walk over to the record player and lift the needle out of the grooves that the record will stop playing. If you want the record to end, you've got to make your move to pick up the needle. Some things, be it situations, relationships, whatever, we just keep the needle in the groove because it's the easy thing to do. You play the same song over and over again even when you are done listening."

So why is this dilemma so rampant? Is it because we are lazy or that we just would rather complain and be a victim? Well, here is a secret that not many people know. The reason we have such a hard time with change or breaking a habit is because, like we discussed in the LAUGHTER chapter, just like going to the negative first, it is the way we are wired as humans. We are programmed to avoid pain and discomfort at all costs. This originates from prehistoric times when all we had was our wits to survive. If something was scary, it usually meant something was going to eat you. So you will do anything to avoid that saber-tooth tiger. While we have evolved since then, this is still in our programing. When it comes down to fight or flight, flight will *always come first*. Our self-preservation programming kicks into play subconsciously. It is primal and basic. So stop beating yourself up; it's not your fault. Now here is the good news: You can control it. Remember neuroplasticity? Well, there you go.

The first step is realizing that you are doing it. Most of the time we need an extreme circumstance to make a change.

Have you ever heard the old story of the dog and the nail? Here is the gist of it: This young man moved into a new neighborhood. He was on a walk one day and heard a dog crying. When he came upon the house with the dog, it was sitting on a porch with its owner. The young man asked the owner, "Is your dog okay?" The owner replied, "Yes, he is fine. He is just sitting on a nail." Shocked, the young man asked why the dog was just sitting there and didn't move or get up. The owner responded with, "Well, it's because he doesn't find it painful enough yet."

So ask yourself, "Why does it have to be painful to finally make a change? How much pain am I willing to go through?" The truth is, *you don't* have to go through the pain.

~

During our interview with Rande Bynum, she shared a story that speaks straight to the point of being outside your comfort zone and growth, "Two times in my career I have left a job: one intentionally and one a layoff—again, while I had no idea what was going to happen next—but I also knew both times it was what had to happen. I just was not making the impact I wanted to in either one. In one of the jobs, I knew right out of the gates that it wasn't a fit, but I didn't leave, because that is what you are brought up to believe; you don't just quit. Both times I had no idea what was going to happen, but it gave me an energy; and both times it brought me to a better place. Leaving led me to working on Sesame Street, which then led me to this, being the CEO of the Girl Scouts of Nassau County.

"Going into the unknown gave me that energy for growth. Someone once said to me—and I am not an athlete—but they called it 'Muscle Confusion,' the theory being, your muscles start to become complacent and no longer grow doing the same routine. You need to change things up to keep the growth happening. Leaving reshaped me and took me to the next level. I could have stayed, but I am glad I didn't."

~

Here is another question for you: Do you exercise? If you do or you don't, as we said, you should. But our point is that if you are doing an exercise that is easy, you will maintain the same level of fitness. You won't grow or get any stronger. It is when you push yourself and it's uncomfortable and painful that you see growth. It is the same for every aspect of your life, both personal and professional. We only truly learn and grow when we are outside our comfort zone.

Now that you have admitted to yourself that you don't like to fail or change, being afraid of it, or even frozen in your tracks by it, here is some guidance that has helped countless individuals on how to get past that. The first thing you need to wrap your head around is, it's okay to make a mistake. It is okay to fail. Your best and most impactful lessons will come out of failure or mistakes. Remember, failure comes before success.

A few years ago, a participant in one of our training sessions made a profound statement. The subject of the training was conquering the fear of failure. The question was asked, "Who here is afraid to fail?" Usually, like clockwork, every hand shoots up faster than a bottle rocket on the Fourth of July. For the very first time, we had someone not launch their hand toward the heavens. When we asked her,

"You're not afraid to fail?" the response blew us away. She said without hesitation, "No, I don't fail." We laughed and said, "Wow, impressive, as we make mistakes and fail on a regular basis." She also laughed, and stated with great pride, "I am either succeeding or learning, never failing." At the ripe old age of twenty-one, this student has fully embraced the methodology that we try to teach so many of all ages. Truer words have not been said in any of our training sessions or seminars with the tens of thousands of people that have attended.

Let's stay here for a second and really take this in. Make this your morning affirmation: "I am either succeeding or learning." Say it over and over, out loud in the mirror or on the way to work. Six simple words that can not only change your outlook, but your life and your career.

In almost every chapter, you heard Mike touch on that inflection point in his life where he lost everything all at once—how he was scared out of his mind in the most uncomfortable place of his entire life, or went to bed usually very late at night, needing to take something to help him sleep, or how he woke up nauseous every morning. But as he said, failure was not an option.

So let's take a deeper dive, as he alluded to before. He couldn't just curl up in a little ball and hide, even though he really wanted to every day. So he started every day with taking one step at a time. First step was getting out of bed and breathing in and out. This was the hardest part—just getting started. Little by little he learned more and grew stronger.

Through this change, this pain, came the most amazing relationship with his children. Mike got involved in every aspect of their lives, right down to learning how to do a mean French braid for his daughter's hair. He learned more about himself than ever before and found the Oxygen Mask Theory—as we discussed in the LOVE chapter—that we now teach and change lives with.

Mike will also tell you he learned about what he wanted in his life and what he would and would not accept. This was the biggest lesson he ever learned. He realized that what you *set your standard* to is where your life will go. Your *standard* is what you are willing to accept and nothing less. So just like in the LABOR chapter when we talked about this topic in self-development, if you set your standard low, that is what you will hit. If you set your standard high, you will reach the success you so deserve.

Here's another little story from Mike about setting your standard higher and leaving Familiar Misery behind; then we will move on. "Once I finally got my head together after that truly rough time, I started dating. When I did, I had this checklist in my head of what I would and would not tolerate in my life anymore, my new standard. When I was on a date, I had this checklist in my head, you know, plus and minus sides, and I would literally check the boxes off in my mind. Needless to say, there were a lot of first dates but not a lot of second ones. Also, keep in mind that I had been out of the dating game for almost sixteen years. Things had changed just a little bit, to say the least. Now the big thing was to meet people online, which I did not want to get into at all. Swiping left or right, what the hell is that? But one night out with some good friends over way too many adult beverages, I was being pressured to give it a shot. So trying to get them off my back I said, 'Okay, I will give it a try!' thinking to myself I would stall it off as long as possible.

What I didn't know was that one of the group, whom I have known for a very long time, looked at me with a smirk and said, 'Really, Mike Mannix, you are seriously going to give it a shot?' Reluctantly I said, 'Yeah, I guess so.' Joyously, he quickly responded, 'Well, it's a good thing I brought my iPad!' The look of fear on my face made the entire group burst into tears. That night, my dear friends—I use the term loosely—threw me headlong into the virtual world of dating.

"For the record, never let your friends create your dating profile while indulging in too many libations. By the end of the night, my profile had me as six feet, two inches, blond hair, blue eyed, and a cross between an astronaut and a cowboy. When you meet me, you will see that that is not even slightly close. I spent the next day fixing it and got myself out there. Thus, the dating began and was not the best experience. I had no idea what a 'catfish' even was, but I found out the hard way.

"So one night I had my youngest sister, Rosemarie, and her then-fiancée (now husband), Scott, over at my house. We were talking about my dating and my frustration. My baby sister looked me in the eye and said in a disapproving voice, 'You know what your problem is?' I responded with what I'm sure was not a nice tone, 'No, Ro. Please tell me what my problem is.' She then stated with strong conviction, 'You have this unrealistic checklist in your head. You need to lower your standards.' My brother-in-law jumped in, and with a not-so-happy look on his face said to her, 'Why, Ro? Did you lower your standard and settle?!' My very flustered sister turned to him, gave him a big hug, and replied, 'Oh no, baby, no! Not at all!' (This interaction still makes me laugh.) He then leaned forward and went on to say, 'Then why should he?' I told her that settling wasn't an option. I could never bring anyone into Michael's and Sarah's life that was anything less than this list.

"Two weeks after this interaction, I met my future wife at parent-teacher night, of all places. I mistook her for Sarah's homeroom teacher as she was standing outside the classroom dressed in a business suit. Now, before you think I'm totally brain dead, to be fair, on parent-teacher night all the teachers wait right outside the classroom. What I didn't know was, the teacher was out sick. Both Mike and Sarah were in junior high at this point so they both had at least eight teachers each. I was trying to juggle both kids' schedules to get in as many teachers for each of them in the time allotted. So as I was heading to the first on my list, I looked up and saw who I thought was the teacher, and said to myself, *Wow, Sarah's homeroom teacher is really hot!* Trying to be as charming as possible, I walked up, extended my hand and said, 'Hi. I'm Mike Mannix, Sarah's dad.' What I usually get back is, 'Wow, she looks so much like you.' Instead, what I received from my yet-to-be-known future bride was a look on her face that could only be described as smelling something bad and not impressed. She said, 'Ah, okay. I'm Bonnie, James's mom.' You could totally see the big "L" on my forehead—not of the 5Ls. This "L," however, was for *loser*. I laughed and said, 'I'm so sorry; I thought you were the teacher. You must have thought that was the worst line ever.' She laughed as well, and we entered the classroom. Sitting at the little round table in the chairs fit for a sixth grader, we started to talk.

"We just clicked. Both of us nonchalantly let it slip that we were single parents. I was able to use my sales skills to read her parent-teacher schedule upside down. What I realized was, our children had a lot of the same classes. We kept running into each other throughout the night because I knew what classes I would see her in and made sure I was there. At the end of the night, I walked her out to her car. I finally got up the courage to ask for her number.

"On our first date, she not only checked every box on the right side of the list, but there were some new ones she brought to the table that I didn't even know I wanted. We have now been married eight years, is my partner and has blessed me with two amazing stepchildren, James and Julia.

"I tell you this story, as I have now applied this concept to anything I want to change in my life. I have set a new standard for anything I have wanted to achieve. It is not as hard as you might think."

Make sure you use self-love to create the list of what you really want, and don't compromise. It is just changing your mindset. Leave the old familiar pain, Familiar Misery you grew accustomed to, and settle for nothing less. I need you to hear me when I say this to you once again: *You deserve it!*

Now that we have covered some of the types of fear that come with change or failure, we are going to give you a very powerful tool to combat this roadblock. It's two very simple and liberating words. Are you ready? Are you on the edge of your seat? Okay, here comes these amazing pearls of wisdom. These very powerful two words are...*so what!*

So what if I fail? So what if I make a mistake? So what if I look bad? So what! The fear of failing is worse than the actual pain experienced. If you're not failing or making mistakes, you are *not growing*. If you are not growing, you are stagnating. If you are stagnating, you will die. Okay, maybe not literally, but you will be left behind. If you are not growing at work, you will be left behind. If you are not growing in your relationships, you will be left behind. If you are not growing as a person, you will be left behind. That should scare you way more than the fear of failing. It is statistically proven that 80–90 percent of what you worry about *won't* come to fruition, 80–90 percent. If you're still not convinced, here is what some others have to say on the subject:

> "The greatest mistake you can make in life is to be continually fearing you will make one." —Elbert Hubbard

> "When I look back on all these worries, I remember the story of the old man who said on his deathbed that he had a lot of trouble in his life, most of which had never happened." —Winston Churchill

> "The reason why worry kills more people than work is that more people worry than work." —Robert Frost

> "The only thing we have to fear is fear itself."—Franklin Delano Roosevelt

The topic of educating people on how to make positive change in their life is something we could write a totally separate book on. Change Management is also an entire program that we teach by itself. With that being said, we have supplied you with real-world tools in the appendix that you can implement immediately to support you in changing your life for the better. In the meantime, the following are the basic components at a high level on how you can embrace and make that change you want. This plan has helped not only us, but countless people all over the globe.

- Set your *goal*. You must write it down. Stick it on your fridge, make it your screen saver, stick it on your vison board, or put it on a Post-it note where you can constantly see it. It must remain top of mind.

- Set your *standard* high and accept nothing less.

- Do a Gap Analysis (see template in the Appendix).

- Create and develop your Action Plan. Write it down. You must bring it into the physical world and keep it S.M.A.R.T.—Specific, Measurable, Attainable, Realistic and, most of all, Time Bound. If you don't set reachable dates, it will never happen (see template in the Appendix).

- Set *milestones* and *celebrate the small wins*. Reward yourself. This will keep you on your path and keep you motivated. When you celebrate your wins, it gives you a dopamine hit in your brain. It makes you feel happy. Over time, you will associate the small wins with feeling good.

- *Print out* your Action Plan and put it in front of you. Revisit it daily and change it as needed.

- *Don't listen to the noise.* The noise is the distractions. Be aware that people will try to hold you down. This might even be a family member. You need to ignore this and get all the negative energy out of your life.

- Achieving success is 90 percent heart.

- Why do most diets fail? Because nothing happens overnight. We live in a society that is based on instant gratification. *This is the path to failure.* You need to be patient, stay the course, and take it one step at a time.

The Great Wall of China was built stone by stone, slowly. It was not rushed, still stands today, and can be seen from space.

- Don't forget that 80–90 percent of what you worry about *will never* come to pass.
- Most of all, *be patient with yourself.*
- You are human.
- You will stumble.
- Pick yourself up and persevere.
- Don't forget that if you fail at first, *so what?*
- Be prepared for change.

One of our favorite sayings is "One cannot change the direction of the wind, but you can adjust the sails."

Here is what it all boils down to: F.E.A.R. actually has two meanings:

Forget Everything And Run!

or

Face Everything And Rise!

The choice is always yours.

∼

As Meg Mansell would say, "Control the controllable. The rest is in God's hands."

∼

Or as the parting interview thought that Ollie Crom left us with: "I always regarded my ability to look to the future and see what the company needed. When I no longer had that vision, I knew it was time to put someone with fresh ideas in my role. I knew it was time to make the change. It was my time to leave."

~

One last thought before we wrap up. Remember in the LABOR chapter Mike told us one of the reasons he stayed in his job too long was about the Golden Handcuffs? While this was a big reason, it wasn't the only one. If you ask him to take a deeper dive, he will tell you that one of the major factors was also Familiar Misery.

As you have heard throughout the book, all **5Ls** working in balance can get you through difficult or challenging times in your life. Alone they have purpose, but together they have power. I have had a few big LEAVE moments in my life. I would like to share one last story with you and how it took all **5Ls** to get me through one of the biggest and most recent changes in my life. "When I told you my LABOR story, I only briefly touched on how I was able to make the change and leave my prior career of twenty-one years to take the leap to what I am doing today. If it is okay, I would like to elaborate more on a very personal level.

"I was truly the poster boy for Familiar Misery when it came to the end of my tenure at my old job. I was miserable and desperately wanted to make a change. Not because the job or the company was bad, but because it was not what I was put on this earth to do. Have you ever had every fiber in your body telling you it's time to leave— it doesn't matter if it's a bad decision, a relationship, or a job—but you ride it out longer because it's what you know? Even though it is painful, you are terrified of the unknown? That is exactly how I was, basically going through the motions day after day, week after week, year after year. I felt like the dog in the story that was sitting on the nail, never moving, as it wasn't painful enough. What a joke. However, there were days when the stress would get to such a level that I was ready to quit on the spot, but then it would go back down to a tolerable misery. I knew in my heart that I was wasting my life. I was so angry at myself, wasting a day that my father would have given anything to have. I would beat myself up regularly, exclaiming, 'You're an idiot, Mannix! Didn't you learn anything from your father being taken so young?!' I was getting up every morning at 5:00 a.m. or earlier in the pitch dark to head toward another meaningless day. I was wasting my life when there are so many out there dying of some disease and praying for one more day. And there I was coasting along, squandering the life and talents that God had given me. Seriously, that is just disgusting.

"Walking from Penn Station to my office in midtown, there is a church called the Holy Innocence. I would stop there every day just for a moment or two to light a candle for friends and family that might need help with what they were going through. But then I would take a moment for me, sometimes in tears, praying, 'God, please guide me. I need to make the change, but I don't know to what and I don't know how. Please help me. Please forgive me for wasting the talents and time you have given me.' I would hear Sal's voice in my head from one of our sessions in the media room. Almost shaking me he would say, 'Mike, don't you remember the line from the movie *A Bronx Tale*... 'the saddest thing in life is wasted talent, and the choices that you make will shape your life forever.' 'Not just your life, Mike, but think about all the lives you will touch, bro, and change for the better.' Yet, I would then stand up, take a deep breath, collect myself, leave the church, and head to the office, stuck in the hamster wheel. *This was truly no way to live.*

"Like a lot of companies, we would hold an annual end-of-year event to celebrate the prior year and set the stage for the next. As much as I enjoyed the time with my colleagues and celebrating the deserving award winners, I would stand there and promise myself, *This is your last year. This is the year you are going to make the change.* And just like the year before, I never did. Can you say Familiar Misery?

"The only days I didn't feel bad about were the days I got to teach the evening or weekend leadership classes at NYU. I remember my first day teaching like it was yesterday. I had a full class and was so excited. It was amazing. The students were enjoying every second, and everything just clicked for me. I finally felt like I was making a difference, and everything in me was saying that this was the first step toward what I was meant to do. I was halfway through the session when I gave the class a break. I stepped out into the hall and called my wife, 'Honey! I couldn't wait! I had to call you. This is why Dad loved it so much. I have finally found my calling!'

"The problem was that the euphoria would subside after every class was over. I knew I wanted to help change lives on a much larger scale, but the question was how. It wasn't until I met Sal on that beautiful summer night at his house when it all finally came together. Sal laid the story out perfectly in the introduction—and for the record, I wasn't so excited and jumping up and down because I had had too many adult beverages. Well, maybe a little. All kidding aside, when I heard the 5Ls for the first time, as you know, I was totally blown away. I knew the impact it could make to help people and that it had to get out on a global scale. It was truly the best life tool I had ever heard.

"As he told you, when I showed up that first night to write the book, I knew he thought I was nuts. However, putting his doubts aside, he guided me into his media room. I set up my whiteboard and flip charts, and we started to sketch out the book. It was amazing. Everything came naturally and just felt right. Both Sal and I were so pumped, as the creative juices were flowing. You could feel the energy in the room. At that moment, I realized that this was it; this was the next step that I had been waiting for to be able to make a difference on a global scale. I finally found it, my true calling. I found it! Shortly after that, Sal asked me to write the book with him, and we decided to launch Unparalleled Performance.

"Sal and I would meet almost every night, including weekends. I loved every minute of it. I would look forward to every meeting. No matter how drained we were from our day at work, we would both get this surge of energy with all the ideas that were coming to mind. I felt so bad for Debbie, as we were not quiet with all our high fives and the loud yells of 'I love that idea!' We were like two kids in a toy store. We would get together any night I was back in NY.

"The reason I point that out is because, once again, on top of my already-full plate, I was called on to handle yet another large problem for the company. This happened more than once with nothing ever being taken off my plate. Now, if I am being honest with myself, I have to take partial blame, as

I would just do it because I was a team player—always there to do what was needed, never pushing back. What a jerk.

"This time I was handed the mid-Atlantic region to fix, as it was in disarray from the prior executive who was managing it. What this meant was, I would need to spend at least two to three days every week in DC for over eighteen months. I would get up, take a train into Penn, and then take another train four hours to DC. I'm sure you are asking, 'Why didn't you just fly?' Well, being the brain surgeon I am, with no self-LOVE or LAUGHTER or LEISURE in my life, I took the train so that I could keep working and not lose time while traveling. Talk about a glutton for punishment and not using LEISURE to recharge, even for a few minutes on a flight. This took a real toll on my physical and mental health. Not to mention took me away from my family and hurting them again as well. It was like a scene out of the movie *Groundhog Day*. What was it going to take for me to finally *leave*?

"Well, here it is. The final piece was Covid-19 took a massive toll on every company worldwide. My former company was no exception and was laying a lot of people off. Doing this was killing me, as I had to make the decision on hundreds of people: who got to keep their job and who didn't. This was the exact opposite of what I was meant to do. It finally came to the point where they started looking at my direct management team for deeper cuts. I was planning to leave to go full time with our company, Unparalleled Performance, and bring the 5Ls to the world—but not for another four or five months. I could not in good conscience let someone lose their job when I was planning to leave in a few months. I would never be able to look at myself in the mirror if I let that happen. So I spoke to my wife about it.

She looked at me and a smile came over her face. She said, 'This is your sign. It's time.' She was right, and I knew it instantly down in my core. I will never forget that moment and the feeling of relief that came over me.

"My next call was to Sal. I explained all the recent events at work and my conversation with my wife. And Sal, being the amazing support he is, replied, 'I got your back, brother. Whatever decision you make, we are in this together!'

"But now I had to resign. I remember the night before not being able to sleep, laying wide awake in the dark staring at the ceiling, with every thought you could imagine running through my head. This was a huge leap of faith. I had two kids in college with big tuition bills, not to mention all our other monetary responsibilities. What if I fail? Oh my God, what if I fail? Even though my wife had a great job, she also had my two stepchildren, James and Julia, in college. Oh, by the way, there was this little thing like a global pandemic going on. Talk about facing your fear of the unknown. But I knew deep down this was the right move.

"When I got on the phone the next day with the COO and CEO of the company, my mouth went totally dry from nerves. It was not an easy or short conversation, as you can imagine. Don't forget, I was there for over two decades, was an Executive Board Member, and had a lot of responsibility. I thought my heart was going to come out of my chest for most of it. However, at the end of the conversation, right before we got off the call, my CEO asked me something I will never forget: 'Mike, I just need to know...are you running to something or away from something?' Wow, what a profound question. It just felt so right when I responded, 'I'm running to something, something that is good for me and good for my family. Something I have never been so passionate about before in my life.' At that moment, I realized that I was using all 5Ls: LOVE. I finally had enough self-love and the right people in my life to make the change. LAUGHTER. I was using the power of positive thinking, practicing an attitude of gratitude, and finally not taking myself too seriously. LABOR. I was working on something that gave me true passion and purpose for the first time. LEISURE. This was my time in life, Mike's true Me Time, baby! LEAVE. I had finally conquered my fear of failure and the unknown and knew when to adjust the sails and change course.

"I can honestly say without hesitation that I have never been so happy in all my career. I cannot describe what it feels like when we have someone come up to us after one of our trainings or speeches, and say, 'I cried so many times. You don't know how much this helped me. I needed this so much! You have changed my life. Thank you!' And that is one small example of the incredible power of the 5Ls.

Dad, if you are listening, I'm so very sorry it took so long. I *finally* truly understand. *I get it now.* I have now adjusted my sails, changed course, and I'm finally changing lives for the better. I only wish I could have said this to you in person. Thank you for all your guidance and patience with me, Dad. Words can never describe how much I miss and love you."

Here is the final 5Ls Self-Assessment Tool for you. Answer yes or no to these ten simple questions as honestly as you can. If the question is something you are on the fence about or have just somewhat in your life, then the answer should be "No." If you have less than seven "Yes" answers, that is an indicator that you need to work on this particular "L" to find your 5Ls balance.

LEAVE

"Y"	"N"	
		Do I know when to leave or when it is over?
		Do I realize I can conquer my fear of failure?
		Do I embrace change and the unknown?
		Do I learn from my past mistakes and move on?
		Do I realize brighter days are coming?
		Do I truly know when to pivot and walk away from a bad decision?
		Do I realize when I am stuck in familiar misery?
		Do I believe that 80 - 90% of what I am worrying about will not happen?
		Do I focus on taking action instead of worry?
		Do I realize that I can only control the controllable?

SUMMARY

All of our trainings, seminars, and speeches are very interactive, and we have a lot of engagement with the participants. Sal and I do an exercise called "Pick Your 'L'" at the end of our trainings, after the group has a full grasp of all 5Ls. Keep in mind, we have the room broken up into five teams. Sal will walk up to each table one by one, and they have to pick a card out of his hand. Each card has one of the 5Ls on it, and they can't see it until they flip it over. Whatever card the team gets, they have to talk as a group, then come back and present one story on how that "L" got them through a difficult or challenging time. This story can either be personal or professional. Every time we do this exercise, almost every team will come back with a very deep personal story, sometimes bringing the presenter and the attendees to tears. We cannot put into words how profound the power of the 5Ls is to help change lives for the better, until you see it in action. To this day it still leaves us in awe.

So if you will indulge us, let's do one last exercise that should be a visual for you to tie the entire concept of the 5Ls together. Hold up your right hand. Each finger represents one of the Ls: LOVE-LAUGHER-LABOR-LEISURE-LEAVE. Now take your left hand, hold it up, then clasp your hands together, and intertwine your fingers as the 5Ls overlap. This is all 5Ls working in balance.

BALANCE

LOVE

LEAVE   LAUGHTER

5Ls

LEISURE   LABOR

If you try to pull them apart it is very difficult. When you have all 5Ls firing in a balanced way, you are strong. If you start to release your fingers one at a time, you can pull your hands apart much easier. It is when you only have one, two, or even three of the **Ls** working in your life that things fall apart. Remember, alone they have purpose; together they have power.

Utilizing all 5Ls in balance can get you through any difficult time you might be facing. As Gloria Greco stated, "A few years ago, I had to take on an additional role on top of my current position. It pushed me outside of my comfort zone. I needed to have LOVE for my very capable team and the support of my partner; LAUGHTER to deal with stress; LABOR in a new role and grow at the same time; LEISURE valuing any personal time I had; and LEAVING the day-to-day of my old role while I took this position on. I was using all 5Ls."

As Candice Corby said so perfectly, "Balance is a choice, and you have to choose it."

The gift of a balanced and successful personal and professional life is now yours.

LIVE THE BALANCE!

ALWAYS BET ON YOURSELF TO WIN!

EPILOGUE

I wrote the intro to this book when Mike first suggested I write a book on the 5Ls. Mike sort of brought them to life even though I had been living with them since 1987. His passion and enthusiasm for the simplicity and the efficacy of the 5Ls gave it new life. But I have to tell you, as I have been pondering the 5Ls, the real inventor of having LOVE-LAUGHTER-LABOR-LEISURE-LEAVE in a balanced way in your everyday life was my father, Salvatore Santo LaGreca.

Dad lived the 5Ls in such a perfect way, and he didn't even know it. I thought of the 5Ls as a way of describing success as a leader, and as we discovered in our interviews for the book, it truly is effective in achieving success. But as a daily way of living, Dad nailed it: true LOVE for his family, and understanding the need to take care of himself so he could constantly be there and provide for us.

You want to talk about LAUGHTER; my mom used to always say to my dad, "Sal, can't you be serious for a second? You are always being the funny guy." He wasn't always silly; he just genuinely was a happy person giving off positive, happy thoughts all the time and never took himself too seriously.

You want to talk about LABOR; Dad was the owner of a butcher shop in the Bronx, New York. He was up before five in the morning going to the market to select the meats, then to the store to open at seven, and closing the store at seven in the evening—six days a week. Never once did I hear him complain about it. Not once. I remember one time in a terrible New York blizzard he tried to walk to the Bronx from our house in Flushing, New York. Now, anyone who knows the New York boroughs will tell you that you can't walk to the Bronx from Queens, as you would have to walk over a bridge that did not allow pedestrians. Pop got close before some Good Samaritan in a truck picked him up and drove him to the butcher shop.

LEISURE, as we call it your Me Time, isn't just for taking a vacation or time off. As a sole proprietor, the butcher shop came first. That's not to say Dad didn't have his own version of Me Time. He most certainly did, that one day a week. Sunday was his leisure day, or his Me Time. Watching him walk around the house in his butcher white pants and a tee shirt and cook on Sundays was some of the best times around our house. Dad taking charge of the food and the cooking, giving Mom a rest, and seeing that smile on his face as he took a swig from a cold bottle of Miller High Life beer, was priceless.

Okay, so now let's talk about LEAVE. As you know, *leave* has different meanings to different people. *Leave* doesn't necessarily mean walking away or getting away from a relationship or a work situation; it also means being able to know when to pivot. Being able to make a change or, as we say, adjust your sails to maximize the wind as it changes, and to manage the change. So Pop successfully operated the Bronx butcher shop for nearly forty years. And as part of life, we all know everything does go through changes. As the neighborhood demographics changed, so did its surroundings.

As a small-business owner, Dad saw the writing on the wall as the big food chains started to enter the Bronx neighborhood and the steady, devoted customers one by one stopped shopping at Jack's Meat Market. Time to pivot, adjust the sails, shut the lights, and lock that door one last time. Pop sold the shop in time to enjoy a comfortable life with my mom in sunny Florida.

One final thought regarding Pop and the 5Ls: As I mentioned in the LABOR chapter, Mom passed away much too soon, at the young age of seventy, in 1989. Pop went on exactly how I described him until the day he passed away in 2010, at the age of ninety-one. You want to talk about an exit, a true *Leave* moment. Leave it to Pop to show us all how to leave in style.

We all had said our goodbyes at the hospital in Florida, and we all had our LEAVE moments with him, hugging and kissing him, and telling him how much we loved him. Pop said his goodbyes as well and told us all to leave, not to worry, and to get home safe. We all left the hospital and said we would see him the next day. The next morning, before any of us would get to the hospital, Pop passed away. The story we were told by his attending nurse was that his vital signs that morning were not good and that he was failing. She told him that she needed to get the doctor and that she would be right back. Well, he asked her before she left the room if she had children. She said yes, she did. He then told her to "Make sure you love them and that they know you love them. You need to tell them you love them." He then asked her to lower his headrest. She lowered it and left the room. When she returned he had passed away. His last thoughts were about LOVE. *Without it all else fails.*

APPENDIX

The topic of educating people on how to make positive change in their life is something on which we could write a totally separate book. Change Management is also an entire program that we teach by itself, as we mentioned in the LEAVE chapter.

Here are some proven tools that are the basic components at a high level for change that you can implement immediately. These tools have helped make change not only for us but for all our training attendees on a global basis. We are always here to help and would be happy to discuss how we can support you, your friends, your family, organization, or company.

The first place you have to start to make real change in your life is a tool we call a GAP Analysis. (sample below) This is how you do it: Take a blank page. On the left-hand side, write the words "Current State." This is who or where you are today. Now, to be clear, you can use this for any change. So it can be a team at work, a company, or a goal you are looking to achieve. But for the sake of keeping it simple, let's keep it about you right now. On the right-hand side of the page, write the words "Future State." This is the person you want to be. Now, in the center of the page, write the word "GAP." Under the word "GAP," list in descending order all the characteristics the future you embodies that the current you does not have. So, for example, let's pick on me. If Mike wanted to become a public speaker, you would list in the "GAP" section all the things that Future Mike has that Current Mike does not. Some examples would be: comfortable on stage, has a strong stage presence, able to speak in front of large crowds, is confident, exudes energy, is knowledgeable, is seen as an expert, and so on.

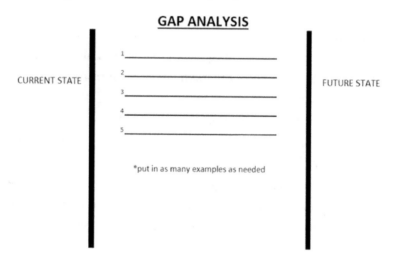

GAP ANALYSIS

CURRENT STATE

1 _____

2 _____

3 _____

4 _____

5 _____

FUTURE STATE

*put in as many examples as needed

Once you have completed this, the next step is to create a Change Management Action and Development Plan. (sample below) Now, if you google this term, you will get hundreds of results, some plans being pages and pages long. I created a plan format seventeen years ago and have used it ever since. The bottom line is, it is simple. Why? Because if something is not simple you won't use it.

Change Management Action Plan								
Column 1			**Column 2**			**Column 3**		
Action	**Date**		**Action**	**Date**		**Action**	**Date**	
1		6			11			
2		7			12			
3		8			13			
4		9			14			
5		10			15			

So this is how it works: You will see that it is broken up into three columns. In Column 1, you will see the numbers 1–5, a section to write the action, and a date section.

Column 2 will be 6–10; and Column 3, 11–15. Actions 1–10 should be your short-term goals; 11–15 should be your long-term goals. You need both to stay motivated: short-term, as you need to feel movement right away, and long-term so you have an endgame. Your plan needs to be S.M.A.R.T.— Specific, Measurable, Attainable, Realistic and, most of all, Time Bound. If you don't set reachable dates, it will never happen. When you put the date, they need to be specific dates, meaning, don't put down "September." If you put that down, when in September will you do it? Most likely you will wait till the last day of the month.

It is also critically important that they are realistic goals. This is why most diets fail. You can't say "Oh no, my reunion is next week and I need to lose fifty pounds." It won't happen. Okay, let's continue. Use your list from the GAP Analysis to create your actions. So using the prior example for being comfortable on stage, your action could be to take a public speaking course by September 15. You do this for all action sections one through fifteen.

Now here is the key and is a must if you want to be successful. After you accomplish five actions, you must celebrate. Do something to treat yourself. When you do this, a neurotransmitter called dopamine gets released in your brain. We like dopamine; it makes us feel good. You will start to crave completing the actions, as there is a reward after every five. Now don't get yourself in trouble with your significant other by going out and buying something crazy for yourself as a reward and then say to them, "Mike and Sal told me to." We promise you, it won't fly.

Another powerful tool we teach is the use of "Micro-habits." Micro-habits are just what they sound like. It's making small changes that eventually become a habit. For example, say you wanted to start getting up at 7:00 a.m. instead of 9:00 a.m. You start by getting up at 8:30, do that for a while, then start getting up at 8:00, and so on until you are at your goal. This is a very basic example, but you can apply this methodology to any change you want to make in your life.

ACKNOWLEDGMENTS

This book would not have been possible without God's guidance, along with the encouragement and support of Sal's partner, Debbie (who brought Sal and Mike together), and Sal's incredibly supportive family; Mike's wife, Bonnie, and his children, Michael and Sarah, and stepchildren, James and Julia. It kept Mike going every day and was the inspiration to make the leap to use all 5Ls and follow his dream of changing lives full-time.

This project came to fruition with the unwavering commitment and hands-on expertise of our publisher and sherpa, Dominick (Dom Details) Domasky, founder of Motivation Champs. Also, the incredible attention to detail of our editor, Cac Stiner. Thank you both for your patience with our passion for perfection of a book that will be life altering. Oh, by the way, Cac, final tally—you did win!

We want to offer a very special thanks to all the incredible individuals that agreed to be interviewed for our book and adding their wisdom to the 5Ls message: Sam and Regina Bei, Rande Bynum, Richard Catalano, Candice Corby, Ollie Crom, Gloria Greco, Jim Heekin, Winston Henderson, Tommy John, Sean MacFarland, Meg Mansell, and David Perkins.

Special thanks to the team: Stacy Zuniga, who was brave enough to be the first to join the Unparalleled Performance team and who makes our social media such a huge success. Jawaun "Jaws" Neal, whose dedication to the pursuit of perfection with our manuscripts and training materials is unmatched. Jawaun could not do what he does without the never-ending support of Joe Olivo and David Erfanian.

Finally, nothing would be worth doing without our extended families and their belief and support in our mission to bring the 5Ls to the world. We would also be remiss if we did not thank all our dear friends who have been our cheerleaders, pushing us forward.

Mike would like to take a quick moment to thank all his friends at SPS. He could not be doing what he is doing today without the experience he gained and friendships made over the years. Special mention to Dr. Paul Ortega, who helped him realize his dream of teaching outside the corporate world by making the introductions to the NYU leadership and believing in his talent to change people's lives for the better.

Special shout-out to Mike's dog, Finn, who warmly greeted Sal every time we worked on our project. Stay tuned Finn; there's an illustrated children's book coming out about you and the 5Ls.

And a final message to the rest of the world. We truly hope that the 5Ls will make an impact in your life. We also hope you see we are not preaching or telling you that we have it all going on. We have made many mistakes in our lives as a result of not focusing on our own 5Ls balance. It's when you are only focused on a few that life begins to unravel. The 5Ls is truly the pathway to help you navigate through life's challenging times to achieve true work-life balance. Work every day on finding a proper balance of these 5Ls, as none of them can stand alone. Remember, alone they have purpose, but together they have power.

Life is a journey with ups and downs, and you must continuously work at your balance. As Candice Corby so wisely said, "You must choose your **5Ls** balance every day; no one is going to give it to you. Balance is a choice."

Writing this book, *The* **5Ls**–*The Gift of a Balanced Life,* was truly a labor of love and our gift to you.

NOTES

The notes that follow offer a partial list of the scientific papers and other references that we have relied on and that you might find helpful if you want to learn more about some of the science behind The 5Ls. If we cited every paper referenced or sources, the list would come to thousands of entries, but here's a start.

Chapter 1: LOVE

1. Johns Hopkins, The Healing Power of Forgiveness Karen Swartz, M.D.2014 https://www.hopkinsmedicine.org/news/publications/johns_hopkins_health/summer_2014/the_healing_power_of_forgiveness

2. Johns Hopkins Medicine, Forgiveness: Your Health Depends on It https://www.hopkinsmedicine.org/health/wellness-and-prevention/forgiveness-your-health-depends-on-it

3. Johns Hopkins Magazine https://pages.jh.edu/jhumag/0905web/anger

Chapter 2: LAUGHTER

1. By the Mayo Clinic Staff https://www.mayoclinic.org/healthy-lifestyle/stress-management/in-depth/stress-relief/art

2. Michelle Graff-Radford, HABIT Yoga Instructor https://connect.mayoclinic.org/blog/living-with-mild-cognitive-impairment-mci/newsfeed-post/laughter-is-the-best-medicine

3. Mayo Clinic Mayo Mindfulness: The health benefit of laughter, Dana Sparks 2018 https://newsnetwork.mayoclinic.org/discussion/mayo-mindfulness-the-health-benefit-of-laughter

4. Mayo Clinic, Positive thinking: Stop negative self-talk to reduce stress https://www.mayoclinic.org/healthy-lifestyle/stress-management/in-depth/positive-thinking/art-20043950

5. LOMA LINDA University, Health Laughter: A fool-proof prescription, Janelle Ringer 2019 https://news.llu.edu/research/laughter-fool-proof-prescription

6. Dr. Albert Mehrabian – Communication Pyramid – UCLA Life Sciences Psychology, https://www.pshy.ucla.edu/faculty/Mehrabian

7. November 17, 2000 Source: University Of Maryland Medical Center https://www.sciencedaily.com/releases

8. Laughter Boosts Immune System and Helps Fight Cancer, Dr. Keith Nemec https://www.totalhealthinstitute.com/laughter-is-good-medicine/

9. Benefits of Laughter, Jack Canfield https://theteenmentor.com/2019/07/04/10-benefits-of-laughter-by-jack-canfield

10. Touro College and University System - The Science Journal of the Lander College of Arts and Sciences Vol.6, 2012 https://touroscholar.touro.edu

11. Stephanie Watson https://www.health.harvard.edu/mind-and-mood/feel-good-hormones-how-they-affect-your-mind-mood-and-body

12. Harvard Gazette The Power of Thanks https://news.harvard.edu/gazette/story/2013/03/the-power-of-thanks/

13. Ask an Expert – Show Gratitude for Your Partner This Season (and Always!)
    Tasha Howard, 2021 https://extension.usu.edu/news_sections/home_family_and_food/show-gratitude-for-your-partner-this-season

14. Harvard Medical School, Scott Edwards, 2015, Humor, Laughter, and Those Aha Moments https://hms.harvard.edu/news/humor-laughter-those-aha-moments

15. Johns Hopkins Medicine, The Power of Positive Thinking https://www.hopkinsmedicine.org/health/wellness-and-prevention/the-power-of-positive-thinking

16. CNBC HEALTH AND WELLNESS, Expecting good things could help you live years longer, according to science, 2019, Taylor

Locke https://www.cnbc.com/2019/08/29/having-an-optimistic-outlook-could-help-you-live-years-longer-study

17. Optimism is associated with exceptional longevity in 2 epidemiologic cohorts of men and women, 2019, Lewina O. Lee, Peter James, Emily S. Zevon, Laura D. Kubzansky https://www.pnas.org/doi/10.1073/pnas.1900712116

18. Repetitive negative thinking linked to dementia risk, June 2020 https://www.ucl.ac.uk/news/2020/jun/repetitive-negative-thinking-linked-dementia-risk

19. Harvard School of Public Health, How social media's toxic content sends teens into 'a dangerous spiral', 2021 https://www.hsph.harvard.edu/news/features/how-social-medias-toxic-content-sends-teens-into-a-dangerous-spiral

20. 30 Benefits of Humor at Work https://www.humorthatworks.com/benefits/30-benefits-of-humor-at-work

21. Getting Serious About Workplace Humor", Martha Craumer. Harvard Business

22. Harvard School of Business, Communication Letter, July 2002

23. "Humor in the Workplace: A Communication Challenge", Robert A. Vartebedian.

24. Presented at Speech Communication Association, November 1993

25. Positive and Negative Styles of Humor in Communication, Arnie Can

26. Communication Quarterly. Vol 57, No 4, October 2009

27. "Laughing All the Way to the Bank", Fabio Sala. Harvard Business Review, F0309A

28. LinkedIn Article published on October 9, 2015, https://www.linkedin.com/pulse/humor-work-place

Chapter 3: LABOR

1. National Bureau of Economic Research, The Effects of

Retirement on Physical and Mental Health Outcomes, Dhaval Dave, Inas Rashad & Jasmina Spasojevic, 2008 https://www.nber.org/papers/w12123

Chapter 4: LEISURE

1. World Health Organization, Long working hours increasing deaths from heart disease and stroke: WHO, ILO 2021, https://www.who.int/news/item/17-05-2021-long-working-hours-increasing-deaths-from-heart-disease-and-stroke

2. Harvard Health Publishing – Harvard Medical School, 2015 https://www.health.harvard.edu/stroke/research-were-watching-longer-work-hours-may-boost-stroke-risk

3. Priceline Press Center – Priceline.com, New Priceline Survey Reveals 92% of Americans are Poised to Vacation With a Vengeance to Make Up for Lost Travel Last Year, 2021 https://press.priceline.com/worklifebalancesurvey

4. Fred Hutch, Seattle Cancer Care Alliance, and UW Medicine Complete Restructure of Partnership, Exercise is medicine, Diane Mapes 2020, https://www.fredhutch.org/en/news/center-news/2020/02/exercise-is-medicine

5. Mayo Clinic Staff https://www.mayoclinic.org/healthy-lifestyle/fitness/in-depth/exercise/art

6. Association for Psychological Science Playing Up the Benefits of Play at Work, 2017 https://www.psychologicalscience.org/news/minds-business/playing-up-the-benefits-of-play-at-work

7. Work Engagement, Job Satisfaction, and Productivity—They're a Virtuous Cycle 2011 https://www.psychologicalscience.org/news/releases/work-engagement-job-satisfaction-and-productivitytheyre-a-virtuous-cycle

Chapter 5: LEAVE

1. APS Association for Psychological Science, Choosing Sadness: The Irony of Depression, 2015 https://www.psychologicalscience.

org/news/were-only-human/choosing-sadness-the-irony-of-depression

2. Psychology Today, How to Overcome the Fear of Change, Gustavo Razzetti https://www.psychologytoday.com/us/blog/the-adaptive-mind/201809/how-overcome-the-fear-change

3. HR.Com, Cornell Study, Why the Worry?: 85 % of what we worry about never happens, Don Joseph Goewey, 2014 https://www.hr.com/en/magazines/benefits_wellness_essentials/june_2014_employee_wellness_benefits/why-the-worry

AUTHOR BIOS

SAL LAGRECA

 Sal brings nearly four decades of executive level global business experience to his seminars, keynote speaking engagements, and trainings. His ability to connect with people, in particular his personal and professional stories, demonstrate his transparency, vulnerability, and authenticity. "In all my years traveling around the globe in leadership positions, you probably can say I've seen and experienced it all. The ups and the downs, the successes and the failures, and the **5Ls** is clearly the pathway to get through it all."

His forty-plus years of global experience includes being a partner in a global audit, tax, and advisory firm, and as vice-chairman and board member of a multibillion-dollar marketing and communications company, operating in over 130 countries as well as launching several successful start-ups.

His passion for the **5Ls** and his vision to reach as many people as possible of all ages and all stages in their life is his goal. He is an Advisory Board Member and an Executive-In-Residence at The Tobin School of Business at St. John's University. Sal enjoys his We Time with his family and the smiles on their faces as he prepares one of his Italian dinners with a little Sinatra or Dean Martin playing in the background, è il più grande!

As far as his Me Time, a good book on a nice beach anywhere.

MIKE MANNIX

Through Unparalleled Performance and their trademarked 5Ls–The Gift of a Balanced Life program, Mike is fulfilling his lifelong desire of changing people's lives by giving them real tools to find true work-life balance. Mike brings passion and energy to his seminars, keynote speaking engagements, and trainings that are unique and impactful. This distinction, supported by a deep expertise in leadership, has made him a sought-after headliner for company events only equaled by the demand for his hands-on, in-person instruction.

He also brings thirty-plus years of business experience spanning multiple industries, advancing to become an Executive Board Member of a global BPO organization. Throughout his career, Mike has always taken a Servant Leader approach. Combined with his passion for teaching, this methodology has enabled his teams to continuously exceed their goals, creating a strong legacy of top industry talent. For this, he has been recognized through numerous global awards granted for excellence in leadership.

This expertise has been recognized by hundreds of clients who have selected him to serve on advisory boards that have defined and driven their companies' best-practice standards for operations, employee learning and development, team engagement/well-being, and customer service globally.

Beyond his twenty-one-plus years of creating and delivering impactful training programs in the corporate arena, he also teaches as an Adjunct Professor at New York University (NYU). In the collegiate space, he develops and administers classes in leadership, management, strategic planning, team building, and business development. He currently teaches at various levels, including undergraduate, graduate, career professionals, the NYU High School Academy, and NYUSPS Aspire—a scholarship program for rising high school juniors and seniors from underrepresented communities who will be first-generation college students.

While Mike will readily admit he cannot cook like Sal, his Me Time is any moment he can spend out on the water, his true happy place. In his spare time you can find him spending as much time as possible with family and friends. He will tell you that these relationships are what give him the fuel to chase his dreams and maintain his balance.

"I am extremely passionate about leadership and the development of future leaders. I believe that the true measure of success is gauged on the amount of lives you touch and leave for the better. Effective leaders aren't driven to lead others; they are driven to serve them."

—Mike Mannix

Sal and Mike can be contacted for events, trainings, and speaking engagements at **www.unparalleledperformance.com or** emailed at **info@unparalleledperformance.com**

Check out our online **5Ls** Self-Assessment Tool for daily guidance **www.unparalleledperformance.com/5Ls-self-assessment.**

Printed in the USA
CPSIA information can be obtained
at www.ICGtesting.com
LVHW021126060923
756781LV00002B/1/J

9 781956 353297